PREPARING
FOR
GREATNESS

Minimizing Mistakes And
Missteps In Business Leadership

PREPARING
FOR
GREATNESS

H. MARC HELM

STRONGPrint
PUBLISHING

Visit the author's website at marchelm.com

STRONGPrint Publishing

Windsor, CO

Helm, Marc

Preparing for Greatness:
Minimizing Mistakes and Missteps In Business Leadership

Library of Congress Control Number: 2023919522

ISBNs 978-1-962074-08-7 (Paperback)

978-1-962074-09-4 (eBook)

DEDICATION

To my lovely and supportive wife, Sallie,
and to all the leaders out there who want to be the best they can be.

A special shout-out to Krysta Rangel for her outstanding
support in making this book happen.

CONTENTS

INTRODUCTION

"Greatness is not measured by what a man or woman accomplishes, but by the opposition he or she has overcome to reach his goals."

DOROTHY HEIGHT

We've all heard the phrase, "If it ain't broke, don't fix it."

Well, unfortunately, maybe everyone hasn't heard it. Or, if they have, they just choose not to abide by it. Let me tell you a story about one of the biggest success stories the mortgage industry has seen in the last 30 years.

There were a couple of business partners who founded a reverse mortgage company. It all started with a $10 million scheduled investment by a private equity group, and each partner personally wrote a $1,000 check to get the company off the ground. Together, they owned 49% of the company. Six years later, the company posted a $60+ million dollar annual profit. The partners decided it was a good time to plan their exit and sold the company for over $125 million.

That was the last time the company ever posted a significant profit. No, I'm not being dramatic. Each quarter that went by from the moment the new owners bought the company until the day they went out of business, they never saw a meaningful profit. If you're trying to do the math right now or questioning whether or not this could actually happen, I'm here to tell you, it absolutely can – and did. Not only did it happen, but it happened to the company I sold in 2012. Had the leaders who bought our company applied the principles I learned over my 45-plus-year career that I'm going to share with you here, they might still be in business today.

After spending six years, nine months, and twenty-three days in the U.S. Army, I began my career in financial management. I started out with savings and loans, which was a position for traditional old lenders before they became mortgage bankers. Then, I was recruited into big-time mortgage banking companies. In the company we founded, my two partners and I did it all – from origination and servicing to forming Ginnie Mae securities. As a company, we grew to be the largest securitizer of reverse Ginnie Mae securities in the country. After six years of major success in our business, we had multiple companies approach us with offers to buy our company. The amount of money they were offering was unfathomable at that time. So, my partners and I sold our company in 2012.

Even though I sold the company, I stayed on for a year with the new owners and witnessed the elements that caused the company to decline. The competition was growing in the industry, and the economy certainly had its effect on businesses, but I narrow down their failure to three specific elements:

1. Changing the successful structure: They reworked our management structure, which had worked successfully for six years. Back to that old saying, there was nothing broken about our management structure, but they were set on fixing it by bringing in new management with little knowledge of our industry, which leads me to their next failure.

2. Lack of knowledge: They didn't understand the business. They implemented practices based on their experience of doing forward mortgages, and that model was not successful.

3. Taking culture for granted: We had built a solid organizational culture they didn't prioritize or maintain. We had developed management principles we really believed in, and our staff believed in them too, which made us very successful.

Aside from the lack of knowledge, cash, and business structure, organizational culture is one of the top reasons businesses fail. When I completed my bachelor's and master's degrees and began working on my doctorate, organizational psychology wasn't even a major yet. The first gentleman who hired me after the military told me all of my psychology-related education was irrelevant to business. He was wrong, though. In fact, my understanding of psychology has been one of the major contributors to my professional success, and it has become a major topic of conversation in businesses today.

Not everyone needs to have a psychology degree to be in management, but there are basic psychological concepts that can help you become a better manager, which I learned when I began coaching executive managers. It opened up doors for me to understand management in a way I never really appreciated before. I started seeing what made employees tick in their own operations and was able to share relative experiences from both my education and work experience.

Creating this culture in my own company with my team made us a stronger unit. We grew from having only five employees on staff to a company of 1,400 employees before we sold, and we never lost sight of our values along the way. Our team was spread out all over the United States. Our core group in Houston was over 700 employees, but we all still got to know each other no matter where we were located. We were big believers in transparent communication, so we had monthly meetings where we assembled all employees into a common meeting space in the office and gave them a complete update on what we were doing and how the direction had changed or was changing.

Good management doesn't just happen on a conference call or in a meeting; it happens when you stop and talk to employees. I often surveyed the staff who worked for me by taking the time to walk around the office, getting to know the staff members, and asking for their feedback. I'd ask how their day was going, what's the most interesting thing they've encountered on the job recently, and what problems they faced that require assistance to eliminate. This makes a world of difference to your team because it makes them feel valued. Many of them have told me I was one of the better managers they ever had because I care about my employees.

That care for my staff extended beyond the office walls. We supported a lot of nonprofit organizations from a company standpoint by donating both time and money. We took a lot of pride in participating in walks, volunteering our time, and raising money for different causes. Each holiday season, we had a party for children in under-resourced communities. We brought in a big Christmas tree, and each of our staff members gave a gift to a child. I was implementing these practices long before they became the organizational "shoulds" or "musts" we see today in a world where many companies only do things like this for positive publicity.

I've always been a contributor to my environment, whether it's on the boards I serve, the nonprofits I work with, in trade organizations, or in the workplace. My legacy is in what I can give back to the world on a daily and future basis. I paid my dues, and I want to share my learnings with you and hopefully get you down the road quicker, better, and faster than I was able to move. You may be wondering what the difference is between quicker and faster. In business, being quicker is the ability to be agile, to change on a dime, and make decisions to better your company. Faster, on the other hand, is what you decide you're going to do to be more efficient in the implementation of your business. I've written this book for you to pick up something beneficial, meaningful, and accessible to your business, use it, and enhance your career forward. My goal is for you to obtain a copy of this book, read it, give it to your grandchildren 20 years from now, and tell them how you learned a lot from this book and what it has meant to you over the years.

Just in case anything I said about encapsulating 45 years worth of experience into this book or my background in psychology makes you think you are about to start reading a textbook, I can assure you the opposite is true. I am going to keep this as simple as possible. No fancy buzzwords or homework at the end of each chapter. The focus is on getting you in the right mindset, not trying to follow some twenty-step formula for success I pulled out of thin air. While the technology we use and the industries we operate in will undoubtedly change, the principles of management are timeless.

This book is driven by common sense. I want you to be able to read something and relate to me. While reading this, I want you to say, "Damn, I should have thought of that," or "That makes sense to me because that's how I've always done things." I'm not here to educate you as much as give you a road map of the process. It is up to you to follow it, rather than veer off to the right, speed up, or slow down. I am going to use simple, real-world examples, so you can easily connect the dots on how to apply the management principles in your own life and business. I am a big football fan, so allow me to apologize upfront if I use quite a few sports examples throughout.

The timing of your journey to success is entirely up to you, but I will be there at the finish line rooting for you!

CHAPTER 1

BE A VISIONARY

"The only thing worse than being blind is
having sight but no vision."

HELEN KELLER

Anyone who has ever started a business or has had the next great idea
more than likely considers themselves to be a visionary. Yet, many
are mistaken about what the actual definition of a visionary should
be. A visionary is more than just someone who creates a plan; they
are someone who can assess, analyze, sell, evaluate, and reimagine
a vision. A vision is not just about *what* you see, but also *how* you
analyze and plan. Therefore, a visionary needs to go beyond just
imagining what is possible.

Vision without action is a mere dream. Action without vision is a
waste of time. A combination of both, however, is the road map to
success. That's not to say the road will be easy. By nature, some of us

are thinkers while others are doers. The world needs a healthy mix of both in order for anything positive to be accomplished, but true breakthroughs are usually accomplished at the hands of someone who can do both. No one will ever be able to turn your vision into the reality you see without your involvement, and why would you want them to?

Embracing the visionary process requires you to first develop a vision. For that vision to come to fruition, you have to plan, map, and execute. You have to merge your thought processes and ask yourself tough yet essential questions. Once you have this vision, you are going to execute it alone or enlist the help of others. If you choose to bring on help, you need to decide what actions you are going to take for others to buy into it as a viable concept. After that, you need to map out each step required to successfully implement your vision. Then, you need to plan for the hurdles. It's very rare that your vision will come to light exactly as you had planned, so consider the challenges you might encounter while implementing this vision.

A vision is not a one-size-fits-all event or action. It does not involve only one thing. It requires a combination of different aspects to come together in the right ratios to help make an individual successful. Therefore, you need to take an inventory of the elements likely to contribute to your success. While you are at it, also make a list of all the things that could potentially stand in the way of your vision. This way, you can get a head start in figuring out how to work around them before getting so deep into the implementation phase that it becomes impossible to backtrack or even adjust effectively. Wasting time and money will only ensure someone else gets your idea to market before you do.

From my experience, I can tell you bringing a vision to life is a three-step process. But before we get into those steps, there are a few crucial concepts you should be familiar with and able to analyze. Too many people just dive head-first into the shallow end of the pool because they are overcome with excitement at the potential success of their vision. That's not to say they are wrong, but the best ideas in the world can still fail miserably if the fundamentals are overlooked. Excitement and intensity will only get you so far before structure and discipline become indispensable.

VISION PLANNING

This may sound crazy, but before you can start planning to implement your vision, there needs to be a method in place to analyze the plan. Before you write the first word of strategy, I want you to be brutally honest with yourself in regard to the viability of your vision. Not every idea will be a good idea, and even those with true potential still need to take several factors into consideration including need, timing, measurement, and assessment

Need

Need is something we will discuss often throughout this book because it is the driving force behind all businesses. If there wasn't a need, a company wouldn't exist in the first place. When you think about your need, it might be something a customer needs to make their life simpler, easier, or less stressful, or it could be a need for fulfilling a greater purpose in life. Without a need, there is no vision.

Timing

Timing is everything. While it sounds like a trite expression, nothing could be more true in business. Timing needs to be planned so you have the actual time to focus on your goal and the amendments or changes you're going to need to complete the structure of your company's vision. Also, timing allows you to communicate with all the responsible individuals so they understand what you're doing, which ultimately leads to an acceptable buy-in.

Measurement

Most companies are aware of measurement when it comes to key performance indicators (KPIs). Measurement is necessary for any goals and aspirations you set at the beginning of each business cycle. You will need to ask yourself how you did on your goals, how you measured up according to your KPIs, how you managed your business, and how you can use those measurements to plan for the future.

Assessment

Depending on the size of your company, there may be up to four different levels that require assessment. The first would be at the personal, individual level, and the second happens within the management of the individual's level. Then, there is also the assessment of how the department is performing, and another assessment of how everything accomplished contributes to the overall performance of the company.

3 STEPS TO IMPLEMENT A VISION

Now that you've thought out your vision, we can begin planning for implementation. In general, some people plan better than others, and some excel at some types of planning over others. Anyone who has ever gone on vacation probably knows what I'm talking about. You are going out of town for a week, but months are spent plotting out the tiniest of details from where you are going to stay, how you will get there, and even where you will eat every night. However, these same avid vacation planners may have a business idea and jump straight into taking action. Would you get on a plane without knowing where you were heading? Most likely not, so pay close attention to this section so you don't end up in Antarctica with only a swimsuit in your carry-on.

Plan

The first step in any good plan is involvement. As an individual, you need to be fully present in the planning process and actively participate. This is not something you can delegate to someone on your team or in your inner circle. No one knows exactly what your vision entails, and no one ever will unless you are able to deliver a crystal-clear vision. This is also one of the most enjoyable steps in the process. You have (hopefully) yet to invest any serious time or money into the idea, so there is nothing to lose in exploring it. You are in complete control of whether the vision dies on the cutting room floor or materializes into an actual business plan.

Next, you will determine the scope. There will be a big difference in how you approach bringing your vision to life based on the size and complexity of the finished project. The invention of a new household product will need an entirely different approach in the early stages than starting an industrial manufacturing business. Sure, the invention can be scaled down the road and turned into a larger business than the manufacturing venture, but at present, you will need fewer resources for the invention than for the manufacturing operation.

The scope of the process is also just as important as the scope of resources. Depending on the idea in question, you may need a team of experts such as attorneys for filing patents, government contacts for getting contracts awarded, or a team of engineers to build the prototypes. Don't cut corners at this stage of planning. It's always better to be more thorough and figure out what you don't need later, instead of leaving something off the list only to find out you can't go any further without it. Discovering gaps later in the process is always more costly in terms of time, money, or both.

The last stage in the planning process is determining the practicality of your vision. Just because you think the product or service you created is the next million-dollar idea does not mean the rest of the world will feel the same way. For customers to pay money, whether it be for a new or existing product or service, it has to solve a problem or pain point for them. There is a difference between being novel and being useful. If you can be honest with yourself about where your vision ranks, you will save yourself a lot of pain and frustration later on. If you're not sure you can be objective, form a focus group of trusted advisors – friends, family members, and colleagues – to find out if they would pay money for your vision. Whether they would or would not, ask for the reasons behind their responses. Negative feedback does not necessarily mean your idea is bad, just that you need to adjust some aspects of it to more closely align with the needs of the customer.

Although evaluation is not an actual step in the planning process, a thorough evaluation of the involvement, scope, and practicality pieces as a whole will be crucial to look at the big picture and not just individual components. There's a difference between an evaluation and an assessment. An evaluation requires you to look at your plan from a helicopter view to see if you've covered all the bases, while in an assessment, you will ask yourself how each component worked in executing your vision. There is no hard and fast rule on how to evaluate the plan. You can use a checklist, flowchart, or any other tool to put everything into perspective because doing something is better than doing nothing at all.

Map

When you get in the car for a road trip to a destination you have never been to before, chances are, you are not just going to shift into drive and hit the road. You have most likely researched the route you plan to take long before departure, which highways to take, where the gas stations and rest stops are, and which hotels you will be staying at each night. Even if you didn't do any of that, at a bare minimum, you probably turned the GPS on before or shortly after you started driving. Why? Because if you don't know how to get to the final destination, then you will most likely end up wandering around aimlessly. You may get close – the right state, city, or town – but at what expense?

Your business goals are not much different from a road trip. The vision, or destination, is only the first step in the journey. Mapping out the plan is a crucial step that will undoubtedly save time and money in the process and could be the difference between success and failure. To start on the right foot, think about all the essential elements involved in your idea and identify each in very specific terms.

As a critical step in vision planning, mapping involves:

- Recognizing essential elements.

- Clarifying the "why" of essential elements.

- Interlocking the identified and recognized elements.

- Assessing whether or not any of these elements need to be enhanced or eliminated based on additional thought or third-party input.

Once there is a firm handle on all the elements needed, it is time to begin laying out the process on paper – drawing your map. At this stage, you may realize there are tasks involved in getting to completion you have never done before and others you might be perfectly skilled for. Anything falling into the latter category is fairly easy to address going forward because you can choose to handle them yourself, directly oversee whoever will be tasked with those functions, or put someone else in charge of the entire process. But the areas in which you lack the knowledge needed to move the initiative forward would be best served by bringing in experts instead of trying to figure the solution out on your own. However, I strongly advise you not to just completely hand over the reins though. Remember when we spoke about involvement?

The more involved you are in the mapping process, the easier it will be for you to learn the skills you were lacking prior and become less dependent on others in the future. Whether it is the first time you've done something or the hundredth, you become more efficient with time. You accumulate knowledge by learning from your positive and negative efforts, constantly improving your weaknesses, and capitalizing on your strengths. After all, leadership is a flexible spectrum that allows you to learn from your mistakes or from new ventures that didn't turn out as well as you expected them to.

Execute

If you've made it to this stage, you might think it's smooth sailing from here on out. I hate to rain on your parade, but if this book is anything, it is realistic. When executing your vision with your plan and the map, the chances of the process failing are high, but that should not stop you from pushing forward. Anything in life worth doing comes with a high probability of failure. Many times, this feeling of failure comes from within you, not from the external environment.

In order to succeed, you need to follow the appropriate steps while avoiding the common mistake of tripping over your own feet. The question will not be *if* you encounter obstacles, but rather *when*. Challenges are unavoidable, so what really matters is how you choose to respond to them. Yes, I said *choose*. More often than not, most individuals allow these mere hiccups to derail them from their original course of action. They get hung up on them, dwell on the failure, and never finish the process. You are better than succumbing to that.

One of my favorite leaders to refer back to when it comes to business strategy is Nick Saban, the football coach at the University of Alabama. What Nick and I have in common is an unshakable commitment and trust in the process. There is no magic formula for developing a strategy; you simply have to believe in the process, and execution is part of that process. Therefore, it is paramount for you to go through the steps as originally laid out and trust you will arrive at the right outcome, even if it is not one you were anticipating. While working toward that outcome, you will learn which steps have to be modified and the ones that should be eliminated entirely.

While you were planning your vision, let's say you ended up with ten steps in need of execution. With further analysis, you may realize only seven of those ten steps are viable and important, and the other three aren't as applicable as you initially thought. The more you work on those seven steps, the more you begin to realize not all of them are necessary either. Although this might frustrate you, you have to keep moving forward. You have to trust the process and keep evaluating and reevaluating everything until you find something that works for you, even if that means dropping all the steps that are not meaningful to the process. Instead of giving up, eliminate what you don't need, modify what needs to be fixed, and enhance the steps based on what you think will work at that particular point and time in the process.

If you are an employer trying to initiate an evaluation protocol for your employees, you first need to identify what you want to accomplish. Here are some examples:

- I want to observe my employees and analyze their effort at work.

- I want to observe how they handle correspondence with customers.

- I want to observe their relationship with the customers.

- I want to observe the relationships between employees.

After identifying what you want to accomplish, you must come up with a way of achieving each of your goals. For example:

- I can listen to the recordings of phone calls to discover what customers say.

- I can read letters sent to the office.

- I can perform a simple survey at the end of the conversation with each customer.

It would be impossible to provide an exhaustive list of all situations you might encounter because of the dynamic nature of business, so these are just a few examples of what can be done when executing your plan. But that's the beauty of having a simple step-by-step process. All you need to do is apply the details of your specific business, industry, situation, or challenge, and then proceed step by step. Whatever you do, resist the urge to take shortcuts or skip steps, no matter how insignificant they might seem. Remember, the devil is in the details!

The point of executing your plan is to make positive changes in your company, so you'll have to resist the urge to fall back into old habits. Habits can be great when it comes to organization skills, but they often work against us because they cause us to have tunnel vision and hinder our ability to keep an open mind to be able to solve problems and be successful in new endeavors. We can often identify our habits when we use the phrase "That's just the way we do things." Those are the policies and procedures that won't change without a lot of work. While habits help build a foundation for us, they can also be detrimental to leading a company forward.

CHAPTER 2

BUILDING THE FOUNDATION

"If you give me six hours to chop down a tree, I will spend
the first four sharpening the ax."

ABRAHAM LINCOLN

It might sound cliche, but you cannot build anything of substance
without a strong foundation. Even the sturdiest building constructed
on uneven ground will not stand the test of time. Too many people
dive headfirst into projects or initiatives, thinking it is a race and the
winner will be the one who takes off the fastest, but that's usually the
person who loses momentum and falls in last place. The same is true
in business, which is why you need to build a solid foundation for
your organization.

CONFORM

You might be thinking good, old Marc has lost his mind here. We just spent the entire chapter so far discussing how to be a visionary and bring those goals to life, and now here I am telling you to conform. Well, I promise, there is a valid reason for that, and the reason is not applicable in every situation every time. But once your vision has made it past the planning stage and is pending full implementation into a new or existing business, there will be instances where conforming to some standard is required. This will be highly dependent on the industry and nature of the business, so don't take this as a one-size-fits-all directive. The mortgage industry requires a lot more conforming to accepted norms and regulations than a graphic design business or a food truck operation does. Whatever the business or industry is, it will be *your* responsibility to understand how to comply.

It is also important to note that not everything in business is cut and dry and not every situation is going to fit neatly into one specific category. So, while we are going to discuss the three categories of conforming and what they can mean in your business, some of the examples could fall into more than one category. We will explain each based on how it relates to a specific standard, all while fully aware there could be other implications and use cases. The goal here is not to assign a label to every situation you might encounter but rather to help you look potential issues in the eye from multiple angles and perspectives.

Corporate Standard

The corporate standard is generally described as policies and procedures related to the best practices of running a business, as determined by management, without any accountability to any internal or external regulating body. In other words, nothing governed by the corporate standard should lead directly to legal actions such as fines or imprisonment. Now, if you flout the corporate standard repeatedly, there will definitely be disciplinary action up to the possibility of termination, but there will also be plenty of other factors at play.

In the corporate standard, compromises are inevitable because not every best practice will be possible in every situation. If the company mandates all phone calls get returned within ten minutes, but the phone has not stopped ringing for the last fifteen minutes, then chances are, you will not be able to comply without creating a bad experience for the current incoming calls.

Another attribute that has to be factored into conforming to the corporate standard is compliance with contractual guidelines. This may include any documentation necessary to the scope of work for a project. There are certain documents a company needs to submit in a certain way to be approved for a project, such as proof of licenses or resumes formatted in a specific way. Sometimes documentation also needs to be submitted in a specific format to be approved. If you are in a technical or regulated business, you are required to conform to the set contractual guidelines. A great overdramatized example of this would be the TPS reports from the movie *Office Space*. Then, there are contractual guidelines in terms of the scope of the project, which includes a complete understanding of expectations, deliverables, payment amount, and schedule. All of these components need to be structured in a way that works for the company as a whole and not only what may be the best or easiest for any one particular employee or department.

Performance is another important aspect of the corporate standard. One example of this is in the customer service area where employees are expected to answer the phone within 30 seconds or less. They also have an average time for resolving customer complaints, which is usually no more than two and a half minutes. Spending more time on a call than what is anticipated means you likely need to get off the phone, acquire the answers you need, and call the customer back. Performance is usually based on productivity, efficiency, and excellent customer service. As previously discussed, these are often called key performance indicators (KPIs) and are set by the company.

Internal Compliance

Internal compliance runs along the lines of internal audits, quality control, and many others. Basically, this is anything and everything that facilitates work within the company. At face value, the corporate standard and internal compliance might seem similar, but the two are very different. Where the corporate standard identifies best practices, internal compliance regulates activities the leadership team deems to be risky to the overall health of the business. This is why you may be given a pass on two or three infractions against the corporate standard, but one strike in violating the internal mandatory compliance may result in immediate probation or termination.

Fraternizing in the workplace is one example of internal compliance. As a manager, you can't tell people they cannot date each other, but you can highly suggest people don't date one another as a result of the negative impacts it could have on the work environment. Even if it's not a manager-employee relationship or they're not in the same department, employees can become good friends and go to lunch together every day, which can often create a feeling of bias and a belief that another employee may be getting special privileges. This is why there needs to be a line drawn about what is acceptable in each organization, and this can be established through HR policies. Though you can't tell people they can't date, you can make internal changes if employees develop a relationship by reassigning someone to another role, another manager, or even a different department. The reason for having these internal compliances around fraternization is to prevent any larger-scale sexual harassment issues since relationships can go sour at any moment.

As a business owner or leader, you have to do everything possible to protect yourself and the business as a whole, as much as you try to protect your employees. There are false claims made against employees all the time for a variety of reasons. Without sufficient checkpoints in place to mitigate baseless claims, you are leaving the door open for someone to potentially accuse you or another employee of wrongdoing. While having a specific compliance policy in place cannot guarantee this still won't happen, it at least goes to show you completed the appropriate measures and communications to inform all employees of what was acceptable and what was not. Lack of any type of policy can automatically be interpreted as negligence, leaving you with an uphill battle of proving innocence.

There are numerous internal compliance items you can put in place to reduce the likelihood of a negative encounter. First, you can have a policy against one-on-one meetings behind closed doors. Closing the door leaves room for suspicion, but leaving it open may prevent any unnecessary malicious accusations. Second, consider recording all meetings, so long as all parties are aware it is happening. Another option would be to always have an impartial third party in all meetings, especially ones where the topic of conversation may have a negative impact on the other party, such as a performance review or corrective action. By ensuring you have a detailed, written policy in place to handle these situations, you are holding everyone to the same standard and looking out for the best interest of the company.

This same philosophy holds true for other business-related processes like onboarding. During the hiring process, you should ensure the applicants thoroughly read through the job descriptions to make sure they understand what is truly required of them at hiring. Then, have them sign each page of the job description, so they could not come back later and claim they were unaware of their responsibilities. It may sound like overkill or adult babysitting, but I assure you, it can save you a giant headache down the road when someone wants to sue you for unfair termination or some other type of possible discrimination. For that same reason, the documentation process should not stop at the hiring phase. Every performance-related conversation ever had with any employee should be adequately documented and signed by all parties involved.

External Compliance

While the corporate standard and internal compliance are both incredibly important for all of the reasons previously mentioned, external compliance is an area where the entire organization can be destroyed at a moment's notice. Generally, external compliance may be administered by some kind of government or regulatory agency. Because most of these areas fall under the umbrella of consumer protection and safety, there isn't much wiggle room for noncompliance. Granted, the penalties can vary widely depending on the industry, but any violations will have a negative impact on the health, reputation, and profitability of your organization.

Different industries have different external compliances, and each company develops its own prioritization on how to deal with those external compliance elements. In the mortgage industry, not providing the appropriate disclosures in a timely manner can result in substantial financial penalties and potential loss of licensure. If you operate a small food truck and fail to meet local health code standards, the fines can add up to a significant portion of your revenue or result in the suspension of your license for operating a food service business. As an automaker, you must be sure to comply with the emission guidelines and safety standards for every state you do business in or risk investing substantial capital in products you will not be able to sell in certain markets.

Whether it's a financial company, a manufacturing company, or a service bureau, somebody will be in charge of establishing their compliance procedures and what they are measured against. This is where internal audits become important. There are two major types of audits: quality control and compliance. Quality control audits are focused on making sure internal work efforts are being done correctly, while compliance audits are done to ensure the company is following necessary regulations specific to its industry. Whatever these regulations are for that business, whether they are at the local, state, or federal level, they ensure businesses are performing in a timely manner and running on target. If a business fails to follow external compliance, it can go out of business overnight. Compliance issues are some of the more significant issues affecting businesses today.

These three checkpoints all boil down to one thing – compliance. You have to comply with the corporate standard, your internal compliance, and any external compliances. Most importantly, you have to comply with the steps you have assigned your staff and internal management team. Since your vision has to be fairly detailed, you must pay particular attention to crossing all the Ts and dotting the Is. You need to know who your team players are and who you will need to work with to gain more buy-in when you implement compliance practices. It is always a good idea to include all these elements on your strategy road map, so when the time comes, there will be less confusion and less possibility of making a costly misstep. If you think the process outlined here is redundant, it is because it is so very important.

INVEST

Can you think of anything in life that's free? Sure, maybe you could argue oxygen or water, but even those are not completely *free* in the sense I'm talking about. Whether we realize it or not, there is a substantial investment made into everything we have or want to accomplish in life. That investment can vary from time to money, to resources, or all of the above. Some situations may require a significant amount of one and none of the other two, while others might require a healthy balance of all three. Regardless of the goal you want to accomplish, the balance of what you are investing to achieve it must be aligned. Throwing money into a situation that actually requires an investment in time to investigate the real problem might result in a total waste of capital. I don't want that to happen to you. Being aware of the trade-offs before committing will give you an upper hand in the long run.

Time

Time is one of the only commodities in business and life you cannot get any more of. Even if you extend the workday longer than eight hours, the workweek longer than forty hours, cancel vacations, or add additional manpower to a project, there are still only going to be 168 hours per week. Instead of thinking in terms of how we can create more time, which is really just an optical illusion since it all catches up to us in the end, the better area of focus would be on where we currently invest the time we do have.

As a manager or leader, you have to sit down with your staff and discuss what you are trying to accomplish. For something to be successful, everyone involved needs to be on the same page. A great way to start off is by explaining all aspects of an initiative in great detail, turning the information inside out until everyone is on the same page with you. Break down the individual steps each person will need to take, and outline the possible challenges along with the possible solutions to those challenges. Take the time to go through everything that has to be done carefully and thoroughly, making sure you involve your staff in the process. Motivation and follow-through are always higher when the members of a team feel they are a part of the planning process, even if they were only there to listen.

Unfortunately, many managers don't invest their time or that of their staff adequately. They don't take their time to do any of the above, either because they don't see the value in doing so or never took the time to even consider it in the first place. See where a vicious cycle could be starting? Instead, these managers live in a vacuum, where the only things given any consideration are economic in nature. Managers in this situation may proceed with whatever they perceive instead of analyzing what they need moving forward. There is nothing proactive about this strategy. It leaves employees at all levels scrambling to react to events instead of being prepared for them. If you want to achieve any semblance of long-term success and sustainability, time needs to be managed and communicated to your employees at all levels.

Money

I have good news for you. Unlike time, money is not a finite resource. Don't get me wrong – I'm not naive enough to think everyone always has all of the money they need or would like to implement certain strategies in their business, but I do know there are always ways to generate more money or reallocate the money that is already being spent. This goes back to the same principle we spoke about in time – understanding what the goal is, then adjusting the steps needed to get there. Too often, I have observed employees in business scrambling to add new items to their toolkits like initiatives, products, services, physical locations, and the list goes on. For some reason, it always seems like an easier decision to spend new money rather than evaluate if the dollars already being spent have made a positive or material impact to the bottom line.

If you don't have the level of buy-in from your employees that you would like, it is more than likely because they can sense your lack of resolve. When visions continually change and it seems like there is constantly a new and better way of doing things, it may be difficult to convince employees to be fully supportive. Instead, they are just waiting for the next plan to be rolled out, while the old one may be completely forgotten. This usually means your employees will do the bare minimum to continue collecting a paycheck, and you will find it increasingly more difficult to rally them behind the next great idea. Even if you are able to convince them this is the real deal, they may be slower to adopt a new concept than you originally had hoped.

You have to know how to use your money to your advantage. Money, as a company resource, isn't all about meeting payroll obligations, occasionally increasing salaries, or offering performance and seasonal bonuses. Let's take a typical manager in any one of your businesses to use as an example. For simplicity, we will call him John. One day, you call John to your office, hand him a project, and ask how he thinks it should be managed. Instead of giving you a response you would expect from a knowledgeable manager, John stutters and struggles to find the answers. You are surprised, of course, because you thought John would make you proud and the answer would be at his fingertips.

If John cannot be coached and trained to become a valuable asset to the team and your vision, you may ask yourself, "What do I do?" Because you are a busy business owner who doesn't always invest the time needed to thoroughly think through decisions, you decide to take on the project and manage it yourself while paying for John's online project management course. This is not the worst decision in the world, and it's a better way of investing your money than simply terminating John and looking for a new project manager. Firing John would have required you to set aside more time and money to start looking for another manager. By the time this new manager gets up to speed with what is to be done, time will not be on your side. However, spending a given portion of your money to educate him serves as a long-term benefit to you, thus an investment of your money. At the end of the day, John will help you manage the account as he sharpens his knowledge of the key elements of project management.

What could have been an even better outcome? Given this is a fictional scenario in a nondescript business model, I don't want to go too deep down the list of other potential strategies – with the exception of one. As a business owner, the first thing you need to be aware of is the value of your own time. You are the individual, owner, or manager who keeps the lights on, motivates the team, and handles the big-picture items. By taking on John's workload, while noble to support his growth, there are now numerous other responsibilities of yours at risk of suffering. A different approach could have been finding someone else on the team who is capable of taking over the project or at least assisting John as he pursued the online certification. This not only gives you the time needed to work *on* the business instead of *in* it, but it also empowers someone else to take on more responsibility and grow professionally within the organization.

Resources

Resource management is essential in any type of business. Time and money are only two of many resources that require investment, but they all must be carefully managed. Physical locations, staffing with the proper skills, software, hardware, and inventory are all examples of additional resources an effective organization might need, and they all require an investment of time or money to acquire or cultivate. Any equipment utilized in the normal course of business should be efficient and properly managed. Routine maintenance and upkeep, whether it be for the smooth operation of a machine or the continual upskilling of your staff, will cost money but far less than waiting until something is irreparably broken or you are forced to hire an entirely new staff.

There may be instances when a brand new system will be required in order for the company to continue operating at optimal levels and keep pace with the competition. Sure, you could keep skating by with the older systems you have in place since they are paid for and everyone knows how to use them, but at some point, they will become obsolete and you may have missed your chance to remain relevant. This is where you must invest. You will buy the new software or systems because they will be faster and better than what you are currently using, even if there is downtime during the adjustment period. Doing so may improve the services offered and consequently reduce the time used by employers on less developed and less efficient technologies.

Imagine walking into a rowdy customer care center with no privacy at all. Rather than having the standard four-foot cubicle partition walls between each workspace and some degree of separation between call center employees, everyone has been packed in around large, open work counters with phones and computers practically on top of one another. The decision to set up the office in this manner could have been influenced by a desire to save money on an expensive buildout or the choice to reallocate partition walls elsewhere in the office. In either regard, this boils down to a poorly managed deployment of resources.

For whatever amount of money or time might be saved by not having to build the space out properly, there are other intangible consequences to be aware of. Most importantly, privacy has not been maintained, which becomes an inconvenience factor to your customer. Have you ever called a company's customer service department and heard the background noise of multiple other conversations going on? If you have, we can probably agree it is very distracting. It's also unsettling to think all of those people in the background can eavesdrop on your conversation. This creates an equally bad experience for the employees who are forced to do their jobs under circumstances where they struggle to hear their customers over all of the other noises. While neither of these impacts can be tied directly to revenue growth or decline, the byproduct of customer defection and employee turnover will ultimately affect the bottom line far more negatively than what you would have spent on a proper allocation of resources.

Not all situations are as cut and dry as that hypothetical situation though. There was a time at my mortgage company when we struggled with the performance of two particularly high-stress departments. The employees became so stressed out on a regular basis that their work output was negatively impacted. So, I met with my management team and tried to figure out the way forward. After weighing all the possible solutions, we decided to implement two of what we considered to be the best options. At the time, we had two rooms that weren't in use – one was fairly large and the other was much smaller by comparison.

We converted the smaller of the spaces into a relaxation room, which housed all sorts of digital media ranging from music and movies to practically anything that helped the employees feel comfortable. This room served its purpose during break periods because the employees now had a place to go sit down and drink a cup of coffee while listening to music for up to fifteen minutes. We also converted the other room into a workout area. The facility was equipped with workout machines, showers, and locker rooms for the staff. Many employees used this facility at the end of their shift to work out and reduce any stress they might have accumulated through the day. This allowed them to go home to their families with less tension. At the end of the day, we reduced corporate liabilities, even though there was a considerable monetary investment needed to convert the spaces. But if the employees were less stressed, then they became more valuable assets. These two solutions are great examples of how you use corporate resources to benefit the company at large.

I realize speaking about what has already been done can seem a little like hindsight and leave some feeling like it doesn't apply to what they are trying to accomplish in the here and now. With that in mind, allow me to give you an overview of a business I am currently starting in preparation for retirement. Yes, I've worked my entire life, and I know I cannot be one of those people who spends his final days doing nothing, but I do want a change of pace and to try something I've never done before. Though the majority of my business experience has been in the mortgage industry, the leadership principles I gained are sound and timeless enough to be used in any line of work, which is why everything we are going through in this book is helping me set up the auction house I want to oversee in my golden years.

Recently, I began collecting antique items from different places around the world. I'm up to roughly 2,500 items purchased through auction houses and private sales. Some of these items are from places like Australia, New Zealand, Africa, and South America. For the resale aspect of my business to be successful, I will need employees to work for me. First, they will have to study what auctioning is all about. Then, they will need to become licensed as professional auctioneers. Together, I believe we will be able to run one of the best auction houses out there. Ideally, the premium made on the majority of the auction items should pay their salaries, with the end goal being to personally realize a profit as well, but I will provide the net profits from this business venture as a contribution to our family foundation.

Another interesting fact is that the company we are going to use for shipping these items has an added advantage – it has a partnership with a UPS store where all of my incoming shipments are sent. In business, this is considered a leverage item. As a relatively new company, I don't need to hire delivery drivers or shipping and receiving agents. I can leverage the infrastructure of an existing business that specializes in this. Even though the employees in that UPS store do not work for me directly, I treat them like they are part of my team. Every week or so, I will buy lunch for the staff.

I remember them during the holidays and make sure each one of them feels appreciated. What do you think that does for custom service levels? Well, if I am supposed to receive twenty packages on any given day, they make sure I receive those twenty packages. In the event I do not receive one of the packages, they would do everything they could to try and track it down.

I share this to really highlight how important resource planning is, why you should start early, and encourage you to get creative. By leveraging the resources of others, you might be able to start or grow a business you previously thought impossible because of a lack of your own time, money, or external resources.

Culture

Culture is another investment in your business, but it delivers over time and won't provide instant gratification. Building your culture and your brand through patterns and practice takes a long time. If a company doesn't know what it stands for, it's never going to be successful. Even small, family-owned companies can find major success by establishing their culture. Though they may not be the biggest, they can be the best at what they do and deliver exactly what their customers want for a price they were in agreement with. If that's the type of reputation they want and that's what's important for them, they can invest a lot of time and effort to make sure that happens. In return, they get paid for their product or service and they can hopefully have many more happy customers at the end of the day. So many companies may take culture and brand for granted, but having a sound culture, or lack thereof can make or break their business.

INNOVATE

Innovation is a key characteristic of any visionary, and it can be approached in two different ways: you can start from scratch or you can build upon an already-established innovation. When you come up with something brand new, something that has never been done before, you go through the innovation process from beginning to end. On the other hand, when you deal with something that has been innovated already, you already have something to work with so the process becomes a little less challenging. No matter which approach you choose, you will need to ask questions to guide you through the process.

While the list below is far from comprehensive, this a great starting point:

- What is the first thing that needs to be done?
- How did other businesses handle the process?
- How or what do my team and I need to do to support and enhance this process?
- How can we improve the business experience?

There are many reasons someone would choose to innovate an existing idea rather than create something from scratch, but the most common would be because they know nobody has ever been able to achieve the best process with the existing idea. If you decide to brave this path of enhancing innovation, get together with your team and decide where to start. A good entry point is soliciting suggestions from individuals who have dealt with the existing process on a daily basis and who fully understand the process's strengths and weaknesses. When all the stakeholders in a process bring suggestions gathered over time for evaluation by the larger group, it will shorten the amount of time needed to get to the next viable iteration of the process.

If you have been to New York City, you've probably observed the large number of bicyclists speeding down city streets in a constant quest to avoid getting hit by cars or crashing into pedestrians. The cyclists find themselves stopping suddenly because a pedestrian didn't see or hear the cyclist approaching. So, as an innovator, you ask yourself what can be done to remedy such a situation. Before you arrive at an answer, you look at what has already been successfully implemented by others in the past. First, people invented handbrakes, which gave cyclists the ability to stop very quickly. Then, there was the thumb bell, so the rider could audibly alert others to their presence and hopefully urge them to move out of the way. There have also been safety measures taken such as wearing helmets, bright-colored vests, and reflective gear.

After realizing just how many innovations have been already made to the process, you only need to ask one question in order to innovate – what hasn't been done yet? This might be where a good innovator would look to other industries for inspiration. Bicycles are not the only mode of transportation where the potential for collisions exists. While the air traffic control measures used for airplanes would not be a cost-effective or necessary solution for bicycles, consider some of the breakthroughs in the automotive industry. Most newer vehicles are now equipped with sensors that will, at a bare minimum, beep to alert you when your vehicle is approaching another object. Some of these sensors will even automatically slow the vehicle down to avoid a collision and eliminate the possibility of user error or negligence.

Though I'm not telling you to figure out how to make cycling in big cities safer, I encourage you to look at the thought process for how someone might go about doing that. Put those steps into action for whatever problem you need to solve or process you want to improve. Don't just look at what has already been done in your industry. Look at the situation at large, and determine if the problem at hand requires a brand new solution or if there is an option you can enhance to achieve the same goal. Lay out the pros and cons for both options side by side and work with your team to decide where to start. Even if you don't get it right on the first try, trusting in the process will keep you constantly innovating. Remember, the greatest minds in the world collectively failed hundreds of times at innovation before finally succeeding. Persistence is the key to success!

THOUGHT MANAGEMENT

- Think of a time, as an employee or manager, when a vision you went over in your mind, again and again, failed to meet your expectations. Why might that have happened?
- What are some resources you currently invest in your business other than time and money? What are some new resources you can tap into?
- In your current work environment, how do you and your team view innovation?

CHAPTER 3

OPPORTUNITY AWARENESS

"Opportunity is missed by most people because it is dressed in overalls and looks like work."

THOMAS EDISON

In my forty-five-plus year career in business, I've heard the word "luck" thrown around a lot. It comes in many shapes and sizes. Some say it's being in the right place at the right time, while others refer to it as the proverbial "stepping in shit." There are countless other variations. While it's not uncommon for people to truly benefit from a stroke of luck, I have always been a firm believer in creating my own luck. By having a solid understanding of your vision, you can become more in tune with the opportunities others might refer to as luck, and you'll discover opportunities others might be missing.

We are all presented with opportunities every single day, yet the vast majority of them go unnoticed because we are too busy being busy. Keeping your head down and plowing through lots of tasks and lists may seem productive and is likely viewed as such when working for someone else, but the truth is this busyness blinds you to what could be. Do you think Mark Zuckerberg was lucky when he saw the opportunity to create Facebook? Perhaps Henry Ford was lucky when he realized there was a way to innovate the way automobiles were produced. I could go on and on about the number of individuals who achieved wild success, not by luck, but by being aware of opportunities.

AWARENESS

Too many times in the work environment, we miss out on major opportunities because we are too focused on other things – the wrong things. A missed opportunity occurs when we aren't aware an opportunity exists, which can be based on three possibilities:

1. We aren't knowledgeable enough about our business to focus on an opportunity

2. We look at an opportunity but don't know what to do with it.

3. We are focused on an opportunity but don't have the resources to do anything with it.

Since it's often easier to see missed opportunities from an outside perspective, let's look at an example. There is a man down the street from me who started a program for businesses to increase sales. He created fliers about his new program, made a few phone calls, and paid for some advertising, but his marketing strategy stopped there without any further review. He missed the opportunity to survey his customers and confirm his marketing strategy was working and aligning with the vision of his company. He had a great idea, but there was no follow-through. If you're a business owner, you know the key is in the follow-up. Being aware of opportunities requires you to constantly look for ways to maximize the outcome you have.

When it comes to opportunity awareness, communication is essential. In management, there is often a misunderstanding of what the opportunity is, how the opportunity is perceived by the management team, and what the possible positive or negative end results will be if we take action on this opportunity. We've all heard the quote, "By failing to plan, you are planning to fail." Part of the planning for this is communicating the opportunity awareness with your management team and ensuring you are all on the same page. If you fail to do that, it's poor planning, not a missed opportunity. You need to communicate with your team and be clear on what opportunities you are taking advantage of, when, and why.

The first step in discovering an opportunity is becoming aware it exists. Then, we can build it out based on the elements we already have in place. We need to ensure we include all elements from A to Z without skipping steps or stopping short, like only going A to L so to speak. We can create a list of each element and review them to identify the opportunities we may not have initially thought of. In line with communication, we then need to share them with the individuals who will be directly affected and get their input because employees always have feedback or ideas the managers never even considered.

If you decide you should survey 20% of each department by having each department head distribute and collect a written survey, this might seem like a great idea for getting feedback. But if you have a department with only 4 employees who are always very busy and don't have the time to complete the survey, you're not going to get the full scope of responses you need. Unless you have someone who acts as quality control to monitor the surveys and compile the information, it's never going to be done efficiently or timely. After a short time, the survey process may go by the wayside because nobody has time to focus on the results. In this case, you began an initiative with intent, but you lost the meaning because you could never accomplish it in the way you originally intended. One solution to this dilemma is to create an accessible, automated survey with clear and concise response options.

When you're working on changing something, you need to get as much input as possible upfront, before you make changes in a process, so you don't miss anything. You can send an automated survey to all relevant stakeholders who would be impacted to get their input upfront rather than only waiting until after the fact. After you've made changes, you should also survey stakeholders again to see if you were successful in what you were trying to accomplish. So many times in business, leaders make a change but fail to get input ahead of time. If you don't make this process visible to your staff, it won't work out as planned. I've witnessed this happen many times when employees came to me and told me a new procedure their manager instated is now taking them double the amount of time, but their manager never asked for their input so they weren't aware. "If you fail to plan, you are planning to fail," is an accurate quote for these situations because part of the planning should be gathering opinions from others to determine whether it would really be successful in your work environment.

There are three questions we need to ask ourselves when evaluating whether or not something is a meaningful opportunity:

1. How would this be good for your business or industry?
2. In what ways have other companies done this before and how can you apply that to your business?
3. How can you fine-tune this and make it the best it can be?

When we ask ourselves what is "good" for our business, the word "good" is very vague, so let's first start by asking if it's meaningful for our business. Meaningfulness can be described in many different ways, but we need to decide if it's cost-effective to do and how confident we are in our ability to make it happen. If it's meaningful, cost-effective, and has a guaranteed end result, it's a no-brainer. If it's meaningful and cost-effective, but doesn't guarantee a successful outcome, then we have to weigh each of those factors. I do this using a 1-5 scale, where 1 is the lowest and 5 is the highest. In order to proceed with any new initiative, I need at least a 4 overall average. If I rate it a 5 in terms of a meaningful benefit for my business, a 2 for cost-effectiveness because I don't currently have the funds, and a 3 for confidence in a successful outcome, I'm not going to do it because the average is only 3.3. You can't weigh any of these factors individually; you have to take them all into account.

Once you know if your process will be good for your business, you can see what other companies have done before. There are a lot of ways businesses in various industries crossover with one another. There are business practices in the manufacturing environment that can be used in sales, marketing, or even scientific environments. Is there anyone out there who has already done what you want to do? If so, were they successful? I don't just mean financially successful. Were they successful in making their employees and customers happy as well? If so, think about how this is applicable to your business. One of the mistakes businesses make is failing to look at how another business did something. If we can transition through their business process and see what worked for them, we can then determine what might be workable for our own business. We need to make applicable comparisons in our industry, as well as in other industries. Don't try reinventing the wheel when you don't need to.

The last question is designed to make sure you are as impactful as possible, so it works in one of two ways: either you locate a business whose system you want to improve, or you take one of your current systems and look at the ways you can improve effectiveness. No matter what, keep the end results of your change in mind and be open-minded. If you make a change for the better, but it needs to be taken one step further, don't be so headstrong in your original plan that you can't make adjustments. On the same note, if you make a change and don't see immediate improvement, don't give up or try to find a new solution too quickly. Progress takes quality effort and sometimes has a path of its own, so give yourself adequate time before you completely throw the system out the window.

By answering these questions, we can ensure there are no gaps in our strategy, and we have included the necessary failsafe to make sure you don't go off target and others cannot easily replicate the plan. If you do it better than everyone else and recognize the opportunity from A to Z, then you have accomplished something from which you can truly benefit. You need to have awareness and meet the challenge for the opportunity.

It's one thing to have opportunity awareness slap you in the face, and another thing to be fully and proactively aware. There's a concept in psychology called self-optimization, which is always looking for ways to improve yourself. There are continuous and gradual steps you have to go through to optimize yourself, but you can't just go from the bottom to the top. When you're doing a project in business, every project has a budget upfront. If you go too slow, you expend all that money over a slow period of time, and you can't finish the project because you've spent the money before it could be completed. If you have four elements of a project to install, you might run out of money before you get to the last two, which may be the most beneficial.

A great example of this is Amazon, which now has distribution centers all over the country. They originally started out with a few small distribution centers to test their project idea, but they may have ended up losing money initially because they didn't implement the idea fully or fast enough. Eventually, someone came in and said, "If we're going to do this, we need to do this all in." Then, they decided they needed to have a certain percentage of all their products in their local distribution centers so they could take care of their customers. If they only carried 2% of their products in each center, it would be a waste, which is why Amazon now has 300,000 square-foot distribution centers where they store a large percentage of their top-selling products. This ultimately enables them to operate more efficiently. It's just like the idea of climbing a mountain. When you're climbing a mountain and have 10 degrees left to the top, you can't take too long because you'll run out of breath at the top, but if you go too fast, you won't have enough breath to get back down. So, you have to understand how to approach these opportunities in the most effective and efficient way.

NEED

Once you have awareness, you have to perform a needs assessment. This is a critical aspect because creating a new program, product, or anything in life, for that matter, doesn't do any good if there's no audience to sell to. Let's look at an example from the automobile industry. Somewhere along the line, it was discovered that it would be helpful for drivers to know when their tire pressure was low in real time to reduce instances of getting flat tires while driving and potentially crashing. So, they put electronic devices on the stems of the tires that link to the monitor on the dashboard. This device informs the driver when the pressure is going down, which provides the driver an opportunity to safely pull over to the side of the road, rather than having a blowout. That was a real-life need.

After performing a needs assessment, we can begin to strategize how to deliver against those needs through prioritization. Let's say you have three employees in a department who need to give paper copies of each of their completed tasks to three different managers.

They are going to need access to a copy machine to accomplish this. There is currently a copy machine in another department, but it's on the opposite side of the building. As a manager, do you pay for the installation and upkeep of a copy machine in that particular department, require them to walk to the only copy machine in the building each time, or make efforts to go paperless by using an application to eliminate paper?

In this case, you have to evaluate the immediate need. Ask yourself what they are doing and the purpose behind it. In this case, they are generating current sales reports and delivering them to the top executives every few hours so they can make real-time decisions on sales strategies. This system requires speed and efficiency so the executives can make decisions faster. If paper copies are still necessary, it may actually be more beneficial to hire internal couriers to make copies and deliver these reports because it will help the overall process. This makes for better utilization of your staff because you are no longer paying your department employees an hourly wage to walk back and forth to the copy center when they could be focused on a higher-value activity like generating the next set of reports.

Sometimes there is only one need, and other times there are multiple needs, which means you need to prioritize. If the only need is to cut costs in one area of the business, you might be able to achieve that by implementing a new piece of equipment to perform a task more efficiently. But if you need to cut costs across the board, you may need to eliminate employees and positions. This requires the consideration of severance plans and determining how to improve processes and maintain quality with fewer employees. If the most important thing to your business is your employees, then you need to find a way to reduce costs elsewhere or truly evaluate your employees to separate the top performers from the average or sub-performers. If you don't have good staff, they won't stay loyal, and they won't do a good job, so you have to keep an eye on what you're trying to accomplish. You can reduce costs on the bottom end by eliminating the sub-performers. If you have the opportunity to hire someone who is more effective and efficient and has a stronger work ethic, it may be more productive for you to hire that one individual and let go of the other staff members.

In my businesses, I implemented a practice inside departments called forced ranking. Anytime I've ever had to make layoffs, I called in my managers and let them know what we needed to do. We weren't going to do it by the seat of our pants. Instead, each manager had to do a forced ranking of each employee inside their departments based on the importance of what they do, whether their work can be picked up by someone else, and how effective they can be. A rating of 10 was someone we absolutely could not eliminate, while 1 or 2 was someone who may be expendable. We could ask another team member to absorb their work or replace them with someone who could perform significantly better. These employees were usually the same ones who were getting poor performance reviews over the last several quarters.

Sometimes cutting costs for processes isn't enough, and you need to complete a staff reduction. That's simply part of managing staff and a business. Another easy way to cut costs is by looking at what you are paying employees in comparison to the work they are delivering. Managers often provide their top-performing employees with significant pay increases over the years, but they aren't producing the same output over time. In those cases, we can tell employees we want to keep them but need to reduce their pay or transition them to part-time rather than full-time. There are a lot of variations to this process, so you can modify and streamline it to obtain the results contemplated while maintaining your staffing levels.

UNDERSTANDING

Our next responsibility is to understand the impacts of what we've done once we start a new project and need to make changes to your departments. If you plan to take four employees from one department and move them to another, their old department, which is now half the size, is going to need to report to a manager from another department. You saved four employees and picked up efficiencies, but you also need to create another two-person department where some of the managers are going to need to pick up some of the work. In this case, you have to make sure there is a complete understanding between everyone who is being affected by these changes. You, as a manager, also need to have a complete understanding of how these actions are affecting the staff on your team. Sometimes, we make changes without revealing the cards we are playing. While it may be helpful in poker, it is not good for business.

In order to have a full understanding, you have to look at all elements of employee management through the changes and improvements you're making. If you don't understand their concerns, how can you create buy-in? If you don't understand their strengths and weaknesses, how are you going to help them develop? If you don't understand what makes employees happy in their job, how are you going to create a workplace where they want to work and be productive?

I have had employees who worked for me, who never wanted to do anything more than they were doing. They were great performers and did the best job in the world, but if I added something to their plate, they were very unhappy and possibly weren't going to do a good job. It's your job, as a manager, to understand that and know when to back off. That's where they wanted to be, and they were good at what they did. This is similar to when employees don't want to take supervisor positions. They may not want the responsibility and aggravation that comes along with staff management. Just because someone is great at their job, it doesn't mean they would make a great supervisor. When someone feels that way, you need to understand and honor their mindset.

You need an understanding of the awareness and the need, as well as of the individuals, the circumstances, and events that will be part of the equation. You have to be willing to admit when something isn't working or when it's bad timing and approach the task with a different mindset. When you're frustrated with something that happened at work one day, you have to understand the employees you're dealing with, where they are, and what you can and can't accomplish that day. As leaders, we tend to want to resolve everything all at once, but that's not always practical or possible.

When you're dealing with managers in a work environment, you have to understand what their challenges are on a day-to-day basis as you give them assignments and have them work on tasks. You have to make sure they are capable of doing what you're asking them to do and they have all the tools necessary to accomplish what you asked them to do. You have to understand what the eventual goal is, but more importantly, you have to understand it's not a perfect world and these goals will routinely be modified or adjusted as you move through the business process. This can be one of the most material challenges when working with other employees – trying to motivate them to understand what you're trying to accomplish and helping them to obtain buy-in.

Imagine someone asked you to go to the supermarket to buy milk. Without thinking, you say okay. You get to the store and realize you don't know what type of milk they wanted: whole, 2%, 1%, skim, or almond milk. You're now standing in front of the milk case and have no idea what to do. Before cell phones, you would have to retrace your steps and find that person to get clarification. Now, you can make a phone call, send a text, or even video chat so they can point to exactly what they want. Either way, you have to be able to modify and adjust your thought process to get to the next couple of steps without getting bogged down by obstacles along the way. The alternative is going back without the milk, or guessing wrong and being perceived as an unreliable delegate going forward.

One example of this is the compensation structure I used in one of my companies. Originally, we had an annual bonus program that coincided with employee evaluations. I soon realized we were missing an opportunity by only evaluating our employees on an annual basis. Everyone has peaks and valleys in their performance that can be overlooked if only addressed once a year. Also, if an employee was struggling or slacking off, we may lose valuable time before being able to get them back on track to where we thought they should be. This is when I became aware of the missed opportunity.

From there, I performed a needs assessment by surveying the employees to inquire about their compensation plans, including the pros and cons. I got a lot of feedback about how they felt the annual bonuses were all-or-nothing and once a year wasn't sufficient. Next, I surveyed the industries around me to see what they were doing for employee compensation plans. I saw this as an opportunity to have a competitive advantage when it came to hiring and retaining employees. Then, we had to make sure everybody would be treated equally with our new compensation plan. From an HR perspective, we didn't want to risk employees filing complaints or lawsuits, so we needed to establish the same program for everyone.

We felt like the quarterly program was going to be the way to do that because a lot can change in a year's time. Many companies perform annual reviews at the end of their fiscal year because it makes sense to them financially, but just because companies typically do it a certain way doesn't mean it is right or fair. Doing reviews based on someone's work anniversary is not necessarily fair either. The business may do better financially in the fourth quarter, so they may be more generous with bonuses in December than in June, which makes it unfair to employees with work anniversaries and annual reviews in the second quarter. This is why it's important to measure bonuses on the overall performance of the company to some degree. We believed in offering bonuses on a quarterly basis because it was more equitable. If the company didn't do well in one quarter, everyone felt the pain, but if we did really well, everyone benefited from the success.

The last thing I did to assess the need was based on a term in psychology called self-actualization. You may have an employee who is a high achiever and does the best they can every quarter. That's what you want and need, and a quarterly bonus reinforces that. At the same time, it allows employees to recognize they are in control of their own performance and their own destiny. When we introduced the program, we wanted to explain it to our employees so they understood the *why* behind it. I explained the concept of self-actualization as part of the psychology of the workforce and how the outcome of this program was ultimately in the hands of the workforce, not the managers. The managers were simply administrators of the plan, ensuring it was fair to all employees including the c-suite managers.

That's when I began implementing the quarterly bonus program. I've done this successfully in a number of companies. Administratively, it required a bit more work, but we did evaluations on a quarterly basis, scheduled the bonus payouts, and documented everything in writing for our employees. For the first quarter, we reviewed January through March and scheduled the payout on April 15th. You can still do an annual evaluation and use the quarterly reviews as a scorecard at the end of the year. With a quarterly review, more employees felt they were being recognized for their successes, and it was helpful for them to see what they achieved in a 3-month period. If they didn't do so well in one quarter, they didn't have to wait a full year to recover from it. It allowed employees to see what they needed to do so they could strive to get the full bonus the next quarter rather than leave the company altogether. Even if they didn't do well enough to earn a full bonus, it didn't hurt to provide the lower achievers with a fractional bonus as motivation to do better the following quarter.

There is power in communicating to employees that you believe in them. So no matter what, you can talk through a game plan for what they can do to get back on track and then deliver against that plan in the next quarter. You could also have a plan that allows them to recoup bonus money they didn't make in previous quarters by performing extraordinarily well in future quarters.

This compensation program was deployed in three of my five companies, and I can honestly say it's the best compensation program I ever developed. Anytime I received pushback, it was based on the belief that it would take too much time and effort on behalf of management. Many thought it would take extraordinary effort to perform reviews on a quarterly basis rather than an annual basis. Another important aspect of the feedback I got about this program came from large companies with multiple departments. They often felt they couldn't implement the process equally to all employees across departments. Although it could still be done in those types of environments, it is more challenging and takes more effort to implement.

This compensation plan was my brainchild, and it proved to be revolutionary. I gave seminars on it at conferences and received great feedback about it. We fine-tuned it every year to make it better. One of the most critical elements of success is that anything you do needs to be modified based on interpretations of what happened. Don't get in a rut by doing the same thing every day. You need to think quicker, better, and faster about ways of accomplishing goals that make employees happier through compensation and benefits. Interestingly enough, quarterly bonuses didn't cost the company any more money financially because they were an aggregation, all within 3% of the range of what their annual bonuses would have been, but the financial benefits to the company in improved performance and morale were priceless.

We had a detailed program spelled out with documentation so any third party that came in to audit us could see the program, and all employees got a copy of it so they knew exactly how the program would be laid out. They knew when to expect their bonus to be paid out and how much was in the bonus pool each quarter because it was all pre-determined. If we had an outstanding year, we would increase the pool, but we always made it a point to publish what would be available. Even if we had a rough time, we didn't skimp on bonuses because there's nothing worse than employees busting their butts doing their job and getting cut out of bonuses because the company didn't do well overall, for reasons unrelated to employee performance.

There are many factors in business that can control whether a company performs well or not, and they are often unrelated to your products or your team. A perfect example of this is companies that created a business based on face masks during COVID-19. Now, those companies have tons of masks, and no one is willing to buy them. They wasted a lot of time, energy, effort, and money thinking masks would be something everyone would continue to wear in the future. As businesses, there are certain aspects that are out of our control, such as the changing of times and peoples' needs. Sometimes, mistakes may be made outside of our department, and if that's the case, our team shouldn't be the one to suffer for it.

There are two elements involved in a bonus program: employee performance and a tiered approach to overall division and company performance. Employee performance is the part of the bonus that should be paid no matter what, but the tiered bonus structure adds onto that and is paid by benchmarks or what they accomplish in the department. If somebody comes to work every day, has low absences, and gets their job done in line with performance standards, they should get their bonus because they accomplished what they're supposed to do in their job. The rest of the bonus is then tied to the overall performance of the department and the company as a whole.

Another aspect you might analyze is whether or not a department completed its work without any overtime or if it met all of its key performance indicators (KPIs) across the board. The KPIs in one department could affect other departments though, which is why you have to look at the overall company performance as well. If the company budgeted for $2 million in income and they made 1.75 million, then there's a certain bonus level employees should get. If the company made $2 million, there's another bonus level. Then, each increment above that increases the bonus level because they're paying the bonus out of increased profits.

Unlike a lot of business leaders, I believe there is a core bonus employees should receive for doing their day-in and day-out jobs. If a person is written up four times for nonperformance or absenteeism, then the best thing you can do is not give them a bonus or give them a very small bonus so they understand they have to improve their performance if they want to continue receiving bonuses moving forward.

There are a lot of other factors that make up what an employee should receive as a bonus, and sometimes that depends on their title level. Most department heads, like VPs or C-suite members, have bonuses tied to the overall profitability of the company. This is usually because they were hired as a VP with the understanding that they know what they are doing and they are expected to perform accordingly. This is why they get paid a good salary. In order for them to receive a bonus outside of their normal pay increase, the company must show profitability, advancement, and goal achievement as a whole.

THOUGHT MANAGEMENT

- How can you ensure the needs of your leadership team and employees are taken into account when you perform a needs assessment?

- Understanding is a subjective concept. In management, how can you verify understanding is shared among all parties, including yourself, management, and your employees?

- Employee performance can also be subjective, but KPIs and goal achievements are more measurable. How do you rate these three elements (performance, KPIs, and goal achievements)? How can you ensure a balance between them when evaluating an employee?

CHAPTER 4

OUTLINE THE GOALS

"The greater danger for most of us isn't that
our aim is too high and miss it, but that it is too
low and we reach it."

MICHELANGELO

In order to know what your goals need to be, you need to perform an evaluation to determine what the current strengths and weaknesses are. Your goals are to make the strengths better and solve the weaknesses. The success of your company is built on the strengths of the dependable employees in the departments because they get things done and will help you move forward. These are the employees who you can rely on to go out there and take steps to achieve the goals, and they will come back with positive and negative feedback to help you finetune your process. You can deploy these team members to do things based on their knowledge rather than just the day-to-day work they usually do. There should always be someone in a department who excels and is good at giving feedback. If you don't have that, you will be swimming up the creek by yourself.

When you outline your company's goals, the process is the same for everyone regardless of what industry you're in. You need to figure out what you are trying to accomplish, what resources you are going to use, what staff you need, and what structure and procedure you are going to follow. Once you have all these elements, you need to test your procedures on an operational basis to make sure you're accomplishing what you said you were going to do. Then, look at the results and finetune the current system so you can operate for a longer period of time with the staff you have. This is when you'll bring all of your team into the room to make sure everyone understands how to implement change and obtain their buy-in.

For example, if you're running an insurance department in a mortgage company and you want to ensure your borrowers are adequately covered on their property, you need to hire insurance professionals who understand the different types of policies and coverages. Then, you hire staff who can write the procedures, which would include things like comparing the appraised value of the property to the insurance amount to make sure the entire value, not just the mortgage amount, is covered in case the house burns down. Creating a comprehensive procedure like this will ensure the customer's best interests are protected, along with those of your company, which is a key balancing act for long-term success.

Once you have the procedures written, you can start your operations with a small sampling test. You'll see how the test goes for about 30, 60, or 90 days, then evaluate the results. These results will guide you to adapt to become more successful and more efficient. In terms of your staff, you need to know your headcount, as well as the knowledge and skill level of each individual team member.

As a manager, if you don't approach elements in that order, you are asking your employees to perform tasks they may not have the ability to do. This can become a big problem because you are asking them to operate the same way they had before without a new structure or procedures to guide them to exactly what they need to be doing. If you follow these steps, you can build a highway that can be driven for years to come. Your internal audit and compliance will be the foundation of the highway, while quality control makes sure the highway remains driveable. The quality control staff can then audit it to determine what maintenance and upkeep items need to be performed so it doesn't fall into disrepair in the future. You do the test so you can set the standard for success.

What you ultimately produce is a higher level of service to your customers. You can create reports and assemble them to inform your customers about your product or service and all of the behind-the-scenes details to let them know you are looking out for their best interests. You can explain how your research showed 36% of your homes were uninsured or underinsured, and you want to make sure they are aware of that so they can get the right amount of coverage. That's your service to them, and that's what makes them valuable to you as a customer. There is no monetary benefit to your company in helping them obtain the right level of insurance, but that goodwill is just one of the things that could set you apart from your competition.

In every type of business, the key is to better understand the customer, the procedures, and the operations, then you can adequately self-evaluate. By doing this, you can provide top-level service to your customers and make your employees happier with the job because they know what they are supposed to perform on a daily basis. All of their tasks and goals are measured so you can appropriately compensate employees, provide them with improvement plans, and determine the most optimal training focus for them to grow and be successful in their roles within the company. When they accomplish what you need them to do, you can and should reward them for their success.

SPECIALIZED GOAL SETTING

Specialized goal setting can be differentiated from regular goal setting in three ways: you didn't plan for it upfront, you realized it needs extra effort, or you received feedback that leads you to customize it in different ways. You may have come up with a process that worked for a particular department, and you think it could work for another department, but it needs to be customized for the new department. Then, as you get into a new plan or project, you receive feedback that requires you to continue managing it by customizing it and adjusting for new prioritization. This is specialized prioritization, more or less.

When this happens, you need to remember the goal is to create a process for the long haul. You have to read between the lines and make sure what you're doing is flexible enough to adapt to different situations. You don't want to spend a lot of time creating a specialized goal that isn't necessary or spend so much time customizing that it takes over a project, but you have to make sure it's effective and delivers what you want out of it and there's a real need for it. This is why it's important to perform the needs assessment prior to outlining the goals.

Sometimes, we set priorities on a business change in a department or company, and we think certain changes would be good right off the top of our heads. Then, when we get into the needs assessment, we realize we need to shelve the idea or go about it another way because it might take more time and effort than it's worth. Not everything we work on is going to deliver the end benefits that give us the value to justify our efforts. That's one of the tough things about management. You have to adjust, customize, and prioritize on the go.

Specialize goal setting is ad hoc. It doesn't always fit in the norm of what you started with, but you know it needs special attention to make you successful in what you're trying to accomplish. It might be as simple as having a person with a unique management style who isn't going to survive what you're doing, and you have to have a conversation with HR so they can provide that person with some management style counseling or other professional development like a course in organizational management. It could be something offbeat where one person has the ability to have a material effect on your goal. If you ignore or don't confront the issue, it could be detrimental to your goal and your company. This is why you do specialized goal setting.

Think about a department store with a makeup counter. They may have only made and sold one product, and they've done that very successfully for years. Now, they have decided to add people on staff to do customers' makeup with the goal of enticing customers to buy different products. The customer can now see the makeup on their face and decide whether it's good for them or someone they plan to buy it for. In this case, the makeup counter is selling a service in conjunction with a product, and the training of that employee can be replicated and modified to ensure they effectively deliver the same service.

Another great example is Amazon. They realized they were paying a lot of money to have their packages delivered, so they figured out how to do it quicker, better, and faster by having delivery hubs closer to their customers. They created regional delivery hubs so you can order something on Amazon this afternoon and have it at your door the next morning. The only major shipping cost they now pay is to get products to those hubs. Once their product is at the hub, they can use their local delivery team or provide the option for customer pick-up. This is significantly cheaper than shipping FedEx or UPS across the country.

Employees are the key to making companies better, and we can't lose sight of that fact. The happier you can make your employees, the more successful your company will be. I like to find employees who enjoy their jobs and do their jobs well, so I walk around the office at a quarter to five every day and see who is still at their desks working. Sure, they may have been earning overtime, but they usually have the mindset that they can get something done now rather than wait until tomorrow. Those are the employees who generally care about the customers and want to provide excellent service to them. Many leaders might look at overtime as an unnecessary expense, but I realized long ago how important it was to pay employees overtime if they couldn't get something done in the traditional 8-hour day to provide excellent customer service. You have to be careful though because overtime can be a sign of a bigger problem. If too many employees are working too many extra hours, it likely means there's something in your procedure that can be improved to become more efficient.

I'm also a big believer in "attaboys," or if the slang is lost on you, patting employees on the back and recognizing a job well done. But this needs to be done on a consistent basis through trust and verification. In the mortgage industry, we tend to heavily praise those producers who are consistently exceeding their goals. Oftentimes, they are carrying the weight of an entire organization, so everyday you give those top-producing reps an "attaboy." Until one day when your quality assurance department lets you know your top producer also has the highest number of loans in default. All of those "attaboys" are now wiped away in an instant because you've reached the point where corrective action is needed. Yes, the employee is to blame, but had you been doing your job all along, there would not have been a false sense of security leading to this disappointment.

SCOPE

Scope is a unique word in business because it's about the breadth and depth of the scope. The greatest obstacle in working with scope is knowing what you want to accomplish. Once you know your goal, you have to be careful of scope creep. In simple terms, scope creep is when you have so much going on that you don't actually get to focus on all the elements that are critical to success. You may have a list of tasks from A-F that need to be done. You identify A, B, and C as items that definitely need to be handled, but you're not sure D & E are something you want to proceed with at this time, but

F is definitely out of the picture. As you start doing A, B, and C, your employees tell you D is affecting the company's bottom line and needs your immediate attention. Then, someone else says you should do E because other companies are doing it, and you are losing a competitive advantage.

It's much easier for the employees working on a project to say the company needs to deal with A through F in terms of scope because they want the entire process to be as tight as possible. They develop the belief that if it's not done today, they're going to have to pay for it in the future. But at the same time, what they can do is take a process they're working through and try to maintain pace by managing the employees to be quicker, better, and faster. Sometimes, you may be extending the project you're working on because you need to set goals over numerous days, doubling the time period.

When you set the goals of what you're going to do on a project, the scope is a very important element. You need to establish the project scope and make sure it transitions to the internal project work effort. If not, it may require the attention of the members of the project committee. It's common to have a committee to manage projects and a project manager who is critical to the success of the project because they are responsible for managing the efforts of the different employees in the department. The project manager is usually not the same person who works in the departments, and most are professionally trained to be project managers.

Once the committee is in place and everyone is aware of what their responsibilities are, you can run it by the employees who interface with the powers that be. This is where you can get valuable input from external or related sources to make sure your scope is adequate and relevant to what you're trying to accomplish in the operations. If it's not, you run the risk of scope creep, which is easily the worst thing that could happen in a project.

When you set goals, you need to set them for a reason. The reason is usually that something needs to be done quicker, better, faster, or because it needs to be added to your workload and you've never had to do it before. You may not have employees trained to do it or there are compliance regulations you need to follow in order to release a product without it being recalled. This is incredibly important in pharmaceutical companies during the production stage because there are minimum parameters and specifications regarding pill concentration for different medicines. If you don't periodically perform tests and samplings, you won't know if the equipment is working correctly to create the pills exactly as they should be made.

When you develop goals, you need to ensure you have the necessary technologies to achieve the goals and the staff to manage the technology. If you don't have the technology, you need to buy it or build it. If you don't have the staffing, you need to hire and train them. In this phase, you need to have a team with an open mind, capable of looking at the process from A to Z. That way, all scenarios have been properly evaluated to ensure all the critical points have been addressed, and all goals were completed and managed properly.

Let's say you have a manager named Janet who was running the tax department of a company very efficiently. Once you are informed of a management resignation in the insurance department, you transition Janet over to this new department, but she doesn't know anything about insurance. You know she's a good manager and a quick learner, so you want to give her a chance. That is fine as long as you give her the proper training to understand her new job responsibilities. You need to support Janet with knowledgeable staff and a team who has the proper training to assist her.

Employees need to feel like they have the opportunity to think and come up with ideas to make things better. Then, they need to feel like someone at the company will listen to their ideas, evaluate them, and assist in giving direction and expectations about the change. There are so many times in companies this doesn't happen, and it creates a culture of followers where no one wants to take any initiative.

EVALUATION

Once the staff is in place, you have to evaluate them. You can't let someone work for a year and never talk to them about their performance. It's vital to have a proper amount of time to check in with employees and get project follow-ups. Project follow-ups shouldn't be three-page dissertations from managers. Instead, you need to be involved with the person on the project, set goals and ambitions, and ask three questions:

1. How successful or unsuccessful do you think you've been on your project?

2. How can you resolve the elements that may prevent the successful implementation of the project?

3. What can I do to help you?

You can ask these in any order, but the purpose of these questions is to find out what isn't working, what needs to be fixed, and what you can do to support your staff in achieving their goals. This is what I call a streamlined management chain, which requires support from the top down. It could be supported with technology or by training employees, but it's important because employees at all levels need to understand they aren't on an island by themselves trying to manage a project entirely alone.

When a customer walks into the pharmacy to pick up a prescription, especially a new prescription, part of the requirement is for the pharmacist to ask if the customer has any questions about the new prescription drug. The pharmacist is also responsible for reviewing the back of the prescription, informing the customer if there are any substance interactions with the drug that could put the customer at risk, and warning the customer of potential complications or side effects of the drug. The pharmaceutical industry is an environment vital to patients' health and well-being, so streamlining this process is necessary for the success of the industry and the safety of its customers. Every employee you hire is just like the customer getting a new prescription, and they should be given every opportunity to succeed with your support, rather than being left to figure it out on their own.

To keep the momentum going at work, nothing is quite as energizing as a bonus. However, it's important to make sure the expectations are set in line with company goals. If you take the time to analyze what elements best fit into the corporate strategy and create achievable goals, the results will become evident through improved efforts from staff, creating a more efficient and effective organization overall. Creating a specialized incentive bonus program that accelerates rewards for those who have accomplished great feats, rather than simply rewarding just them for doing their job, provides encouragement and inspiration to go above and beyond. Each person should be evaluated and rewarded based on their individual successes and merits, according to the company's expectations. Real achievements and goals should be determined by each individual's efforts, not just broadly applied to everyone as an all-encompassing blanket of entitlement. A tiered bonus system serves better for rewarding those who strive for excellence, allowing them to be rewarded for their hard work and going above and beyond.

When I wanted to implement this new benefit, I gathered a number of managers in the boardroom, determined to find out the positives and negatives of this new bonus program. I wanted to ensure everything that could possibly go wrong had been taken into account, while also identifying anything that might give us an extra edge against the competition. After much discussion, we came up with a number of possibilities. We took our ideas and our processes back out into the field to test them over several quarters before reconvening and seeing exactly how things had gone. We found both positives and negatives, which gave us new insight into what worked best for us and gave us some room for future improvements too.

We determined morale was generally up, as many employees felt sincerely acknowledged for their hard work. However, there were still some individuals who felt slighted by not receiving bonuses that time around, and it created a difficult situation. It became clear this was a complex topic – the employees felt proud and appreciated if they got rewarded but emotionally hurt if they didn't. We needed to ensure we had the proper messaging around the program so employees who didn't receive bonuses understood they still had the potential to earn it if they improved their performance. We told them what they needed to do to perform better and gave them the opportunity to earn a bonus in the future, which made them feel supported and valued.

Next, I called in the mid-level managers and supervisors to get their input on the new bonus program. I simply asked how it was working for them. They told me whether it helped or hindered their work and if it had a positive impact on the employees. Most of the supervisors thought the program was great because it allowed them to rank their employees based on their productivity and contribution to the company's mission. This made it easier to distinguish between those who had just filled their role and those who had made a real impact. From there, I took their feedback and used it to have a company-wide meeting with representatives from management, supervision, and the employee level to ensure everyone was on the same page about the bonus program and how it would impact their work.

It's important to recognize everyone is unique, so they won't fit into the same box. Leaders should strive to recognize those who worked hard and achieved great things but also remember those who have not yet been rewarded for their efforts. When employees begin to feel underappreciated, it causes morale problems on a large scale, which is why we need to treat them with respect, validate their effort, and show they are valued members of the team. A strong sense of appreciation can propel any organization forward, while a lack thereof can stunt its growth.

THOUGHT MANAGEMENT

- Think about a time you were unable to achieve a goal. What prevented you from achieving the goal and what did you learn from that experience?

- What are some ways you can manage scope creep in your business? Consider the people, resources, and tools available to support you.

- How can you use a streamlined management chain to evaluate your goals and support your employees?

CHAPTER 5

OUTLINE THE MISSION

"Your mission statement becomes your constitution,
the solid expression of your vision and values.
It becomes the criterion by which you measure
everything else in your life."

STEPHEN COVEY

A mission is not the same thing as a goal. While a goal is something we set out to achieve, failure to attain a goal from time to time is generally accepted as unavoidable. A mission, however, transcends a goal. When you are on a mission, nothing can stand in your way, and failure is not an option. But in order for a mission to be successful, it must be clear in its purpose and made available to everyone it is dependent on for success.

When looking at an organization's mission, there isn't just one mission. Instead, there are three distinct missions in play - the mission of management, the mission of the company, and the mission of employees. Each of these goals requires different approaches and considerations for how to effectively achieve them. Understanding this multi-faceted approach is key to organizational success and outlines why a more holistic view is so important. The best managers and leaders understand it cannot be one way, or more specifically, their way, all the time. Instead, they know how to prioritize the correct mission at the appropriate time.

TYPES OF MISSIONS

1. Mission of Management

A company's mission of management, from the boardroom to frontline workers, is all about getting results. Effective managers need to stay on top of processes and keep projects running in order to achieve productivity goals. They must strive to improve productivity without compromising quality or employee morale. There is a delicate balance between managing the boss's requests and leading employees who are expected to complete tasks within certain parameters and timelines. Good managers are skilled in the humanization of management, which is the ability to recognize their employees as more than just workers who complete tasks. When we view our employees as unique individuals with special talents, skills, and needs, we can maintain employee morale and be more efficient in our businesses. When we implement new processes, good managers will identify value propositions, monitor progress, proactively respond to issues, and set clear expectations for employees in order to complete the task at hand while keeping bosses satisfied with the outcome. With this combination of strategies in place, management can keep things running smoothly while satisfying both internal stakeholders and top bosses alike.

When a good manager in a department makes a major recommendation for change, they can make that recommendation by stating elements of why it is good, which may mean it's cost-effective and it's going to be a better, more user-friendly process. When you do those things, you identify what your value proposition is, which is stating what it's saving and what is being made quicker, faster, or better for the customer. Once you make a change, you can effectively monitor those things to make sure they stay at the same level because everything can go astray quickly. If NASA had not been monitoring Apollo 13 enough to learn from its mistakes, it could have been detrimental to NASA, not only the image of the company, but the financial and life-or-death aspects would have run them into the ground. Monitoring the pluses and minuses of everything you have done is important because it allows you to proactively respond to the issues at hand as they arise. With that, it also helps us manage people as we set expectations for them. People, products, and services make the business world go 'round. Your product can be your service, and your service could be your product. If you're a plumber, you can sell new water heaters, but you can also provide maintenance on that, which would be your service. Employees can perform services or complete tasks, but it takes a great employee to do them well, with minimal missteps.

2. Mission of Company

The mission of the company is to attain profits and help the bottom line in order to meet the expectations of its shareholders and clients. Profit is the main motivation for doing business and is critical for any organization to become more successful and productive in the long term. But companies should also focus on customer satisfaction, cost savings, and increasing efficiency to accomplish their mission of earning sustainable profit. In order to achieve their mission, organizations must continually improve on different aspects like technology, products/services, marketing strategies, and financial management systems. Once a company captures its fundamental profitability, it can then look towards achieving other goals like greater market share or expanding into new territories.

Corporate profitability is essential for a company's ongoing success and involves more than just a financial return. It also means successful positioning in the market and creating value for stakeholders that will not necessarily manifest itself solely in monetary form. Business leaders must be forward-thinking, with an eye toward the future and how their current actions will lead to potential gains in terms of reputation, public awareness, customer loyalty, and operational efficiency. This common understanding of corporate profitability as much more than just dollar signs helps ensure companies are effectively recognizing changes in their industry and staying ahead of competitive pressures.

3. The Mission of Employees

The mission of employees should be to not only be content in their jobs but to also feel a sense of satisfaction from completing their work. That could mean taking breaks throughout the day to recharge or adjusting tasks to minimize stress and burnout. When workers are fulfilled and productive in the workplace, it creates a chain reaction throughout organizations and even entire industries, which ultimately drives innovation and progress. At the end of the day, employees should strive to succeed in their work while still maintaining a proper work-life balance. That way, they can have healthy lives both on and off the job.

Companies have come to realize the importance of truly understanding their staff, not just in their job-related roles, but also by their true potential to grow and develop in practical and positive ways through the humanization of management. This is an ethos of recognizing employees as more than just cogs in a corporate machine but as unique individuals. This shift towards humanizing management has clear advantages. Workers who feel heard, appreciated, and respected tend to be more productive than those who don't experience such recognition. Ultimately, when companies prioritize listening closely to the actual staff they employ and fostering positive relationships at all organizational levels, everyone benefits.

This is not just limited to the rank-and-file employees but all parts of the management structure from the boss down to the second tier of managers and even to the newest team members. A successful team ensures all of its members, from the newest to the oldest, are happy in their roles and performing efficiently, which can only be achieved by taking into account their individual needs and situations. Paying attention to this mission will ensure better results every time.

MISSION AND GOALS

It is important to have a well-delineated mission for your organization. This mission should clearly and succinctly communicate what the organization intends to accomplish and how it will achieve its goals. It should be an accurate reflection of the beliefs, values, and objectives of the organization in order to ensure short-term and long-term success. When creating the mission statement, evaluate your current goals and consider how they can be reflected in the mission. With a strategic mission that aligns with these goals, you can create an effective road map for progress to guide every decision throughout all aspects of your business.

A pertinent example of this is how NASA paved the way in space exploration for other companies like SpaceX, Blue Horizons Aerospace, and Virgin Galactic, who all have the extended goal of space travel and exploration by putting a man on Mars. Before they could do that, they needed to outline a plan for getting a man back to the moon again. This plan involved extensive preparation and establishing milestones to be accomplished along the way such as a number of successful trips back and forth between Earth and the moon before any other mission could possibly start. Additionally, those involved in the mission need to understand its scale and know what challenges may arise. All these components are necessary for planning such a large-scale endeavor.

Oftentimes, employees think they can get results quickly by simply figuring out the goal and shooting for it. This mentality underestimates the amount of time and planning needed to achieve success effectively, but this is precisely where failure and management come into play. Managing failure involves understanding the full scope of what is expected on the journey toward the end result, instead of simply taking a trip. Without adequate preparation, rushing blindly into any task can lead to frustration and more failures in the long run. Knowing when to pause and regroup or laser focus on thoroughly planning out each step will ensure each goal can be reached with maximum efficiency and less pressure placed on everyone involved.

In sports like football, buy-in from the players is key. Every position needs to work together and have an understanding of its role in achieving the ultimate goal – in this case, to win a national championship. When it comes specifically to an offensive line protecting the quarterback, their dedication and strength as a unit are paramount if you're going to score points and take home the trophy. It's no wonder that when they do manage to pull it off, quarterbacks often show their appreciation by gifting items to their linemen. After all, the quarterbacks know they couldn't have achieved their success without the support of their teammates.

Everyone involved in the company's mission should have their views taken into consideration prior to its formulation. To do this, there are several strategies that can be implemented. Holding team meetings or launching surveys will provide a platform for those individuals to express their ideas, concerns, and feedback. This information can then be used to shape the mission statement and create clear objectives. When everybody has invested time and effort into the mission creation process, it becomes much more likely they will commit to aiming for the same goals and working together to achieve them. Using the same lineman example, everyone needs to be on the same page of the playbook if the quarterback is going to hand the ball off to the running back, and the blocking then needs to adjust accordingly.

Having a strong buy-in to the mission of a company is beneficial because it helps employees stay focused and motivated, supports a positive culture, and impacts how employees interact with each other and their customers. One way to ensure employees truly buy into the mission is by getting them involved in the planning process. Allowing an employee to contribute to goal-setting activities or generate ideas for how to reach those goals shows them their opinion is valued and they are part of the bigger picture. This encourages trust, creativity, and ownership, which ultimately leads to more success within a company.

Think of it like taking a vacation with the people closest to you. If you don't get their buy-in early on, your trip will quickly become unpleasant and filled with complaining. Buy-in from those who are part of the mission ensures all preferences are heard, creating a much more enjoyable experience for all, whether this means planning activities for cold weather or booking a spa day at a nearby hotel. Getting employee buy-in is vital for any successful mission to be completed in an enjoyable way.

When employees understand and accept the mission of a company, they become fully integrated into the planning process as well. Their work becomes enjoyable, and they are more likely to provide meaningful and informed suggestions that can lead to a successful mission. This type of buy-in brings everyone involved together in a way that creates synergy and builds strong teams who are capable of reaching desired goals. It's a powerful combination when everyone buys into the mission and makes it their own.

PRIORITIZING YOUR MISSIONS

The mission of the company is the foundation for any successful enterprise and is often viewed as paramount. It focuses foremost on profitability, reinforcing the need to make money and stay afloat. Management's mission often comes second and entails greater productivity. By optimizing workflow, managers can ensure resources are used with the utmost efficiency. Last but not least, the mission centers on employee satisfaction, providing a sense of purpose to working individuals, alongside competitive wages and benefits. Companies take into account all three of these layers when they develop business strategies in order to drive long-term success.

Although the mission of employees often comes last in an organization, technically, the human aspect encompasses all aspects of the mission at all levels. Employees are the backbone of any well-run organization, be it a business, school, or government entity. Without employees to set the tone and drive progress, organizations are prone to flounder and fall behind their competitors. Even though an employee-first mindset may not always seem viable in terms of capital investments or talent management, having an understanding of how team dynamics can positively influence outcomes is essential for success. Human resources is not just a department; it also represents core principles on which all productive functioning relies. By keeping employees happy and investing in skills development, organizations have the opportunity to make meaningful progress.

Prioritizing the missions of the company, management, and employees can be a balancing act, so flexibility is necessary. A successful work culture needs to recognize what each mission can bring to the table and adjust its strategies accordingly. Fulfilling each of these missions in a balanced way will ensure all employees are held to the same standards while also giving individuals the opportunity to excel and grow with the company. It will provide an environment where everyone can communicate effectively, stay motivated, and have pride in their contributions. An organization's flexibility in missions creates an empowered workplace that encourages progress and innovation at every level. An organization must be flexible enough to understand the importance of each one but remain agile enough to adjust focus when needed for overall success.

In football, all players should be playing in service of the team's success. However, there are certain circumstances where an individual player needs to take control of the overall team goals. This is where the managers and coaches come in, as they are responsible for setting priorities and ensuring everyone is playing a role in helping reach collective success without putting themselves at risk of harm. The coaches and other managers need to make difficult decisions by weighing the potential reward of victory against the risk of long-term injury or physical impairment. Ultimately, these decisions can only be made successfully when everyone has bought into them; otherwise, morale could be seriously affected and disrupt the entire structure of the team.

DIFFICULTIES IN OUTLINING THE MISSION

One of the most important tasks when establishing a company or organization is to define its mission. While this step can seem overwhelming, it is crucial to accomplish this task properly because the mission statement will serve as a guide for the company and inform its current employees, potential employees, suppliers, customers, and other stakeholders of the overall purpose. Creating an effective mission statement is not an easy task; it requires considerable thought to accurately reflect the values and objectives of the organization.

In addition, executives must consider how those objectives will be achieved and what language to use to prevent overly broad statements that could leave room for misinterpretation. The difficulties in outlining a mission should not be underestimated. An inaccurate or lackluster mission leaves potential partners and employees without a clear understanding of the company's core values and purpose.

Though it's incredibly important to the success of a mission, getting buy-in from all of the important stakeholders early on is critical to making sure the mission moves forward without any roadblocks. It is important to clearly articulate the value of the mission and its purpose to everyone who is going to be a contributor. By doing this, every individual will understand their role and how their work contributes to achieving the overall mission objectives.

Having an established mission for any company is key in order to successfully fulfill the needs of those around them. A few years back, Lifetime TV's management team set forth a goal to adjust its programming to better cater to the changing culture, which resulted in integrating more people of color and LGBTQ+ representation into their programming. To ensure the successful implementation of their mission, they had to recognize the level of acceptance their audience had towards such shows and if this change would be embraced and appreciated long term.

Making decisions of this magnitude in corporations is no easy task. Leadership needs to take into account the viewpoints of their employees and their external stakeholders as well as the costs associated with them. There must be a team effort to weigh the benefits and drawbacks of each decision, so the management team needs to be prepared to support any course of action. Analyzing which route fully accounts for both internal and external perspectives while being the most cost-effective will ultimately lead to better decision-making and mission outlines.

Mission statements should embrace inclusivity. When crafting a mission statement, it's important to keep in mind the varied backgrounds and styles of each member of your team. You may have an employee who grew up as an only child and therefore works well independently, while an employee from a larger family may enjoy collaboration with others. Crafting a mission statement to support both these types of working styles can ensure progress for all involved. Making sure everyone has input into the mission's creation can build an inclusive culture and prevent any one group from feeling excluded. Thoughtfully constructing an inclusive mission statement supports different working styles and allows for meaningful participation from all members of your team, which will lead to successful cooperation and a unified purpose.

EVOLUTION OF MISSIONS

If you are leading a company, it is important to be prepared for shifts in values, expectations, and external forces that could prompt your mission to evolve. It is wise to stay attentive and open-minded and be ready to evolve alongside the needs of customers, markets, social media trends, or other disruptive forces. Though change has been increasing exponentially over the years, businesses have adaptation resources they can use. A company's mission is not just about where it has been but also about where it is going. Thus, it is important for businesses to remain agile and open to change as customer needs and market conditions evolve. You should evaluate current processes while also looking forward with an eye toward tomorrow's changes. This way, your company won't be left behind as the world shifts in policies and standards.

Here are three simple ways you can make sure you are ready for any changes in the mission:

1. Be observant

Being an observant leader in the workplace can be a great asset for any team, no matter the industry. It helps you to develop a better understanding of the climate around you and identify any potential issues or concerns early on. By being proactive and engaging with your team, you can create opportunities for open dialogue and positive change rather than creating resistance or fear. As a leader, observing what's happening in your work environment gives you the insights necessary to make informed decisions aligned with your goals that will be beneficial to your team, company, and customers.

Trying to dramatically change the culture of a company that has operated in the same fashion for many years is no small feat. Muscling in and demanding instant changes will inevitably cause resistance from employees who are used to doing things a certain way and see no reason to alter those methods. Without proper consideration or consultation, it can be difficult for someone new to win these employees over, so all changes need to have reason and any concerns of existing personnel should be listened to earnestly. Modifications can only be adopted through careful consideration by long-time members of the team and integrated into their working practices.

Once you notice the changes, trends, and needs within this new workplace landscape, you will be better equipped to bring positive change. This heightened sense of awareness may also prompt further insight into how your specific job plays a part in creating success for your team or organization. Being regularly observant will help you stay ahead when it comes to recognizing opportunities to drive efficiencies and introduce process improvements to make everyone more productive.

2. Be sensitive

Working in a team setting is often much easier if you are sensitive to the environment. With each new job or project, it can be helpful to take time to observe and understand your colleagues before jumping headfirst into the work. Taking notice of how others interact and conduct themselves can give you insight into how to intersperse yourself into discussions, propose ideas, and come up with the best possible solutions for a group task. This can provide the freedom to bring positive change from within the team environment, improving morale, productivity, and results for everyone involved.

Developing sensitivity to workplace dynamics and relationships can help you better understand how communication, interaction, and collaboration work throughout the organization. A positive attitude that reflects understanding and acceptance of different working styles, hierarchies, and approaches will foster cooperation and discourse within your workgroup. By investing time into learning about the company culture, norms, and practices, you can establish yourself to be an active contributor toward mission success from within.

3. Be a salesman

To make lasting, meaningful changes in the workplace, it is important to think outside the box and become a salesperson of sorts. This may involve having complex conversations with departments and presenting solutions to help a company gain efficiency and the ability to produce better results on limited resources. It might mean introducing insights from past work environments and suggesting modifications that could be used to create a stronger workforce overall, making for better products and improved profitability. Being an advocate of change requires being able to "sell" these solutions in order for them to take root. By doing this, you can make a real difference in how things are run within an organization.

Making profound changes in the workplace is not an easy task. The manager can take the first step by giving a presentation to the whole group and trying to convince them of the potential behind the change. However, it is impossible for one person to influence everyone in all different tiers, so it will be beneficial to create a hierarchy to sell the change to the various management levels in the company. The manager must delegate selling opportunities to their direct reports and rely on them to do their best in distilling the message properly. This way, unique ideas can be spread among all employees to create a meaningful and lasting impact on the working environment.

GROWTH AND DEVELOPMENT THROUGH ASSESSMENT

All employees probably engage in some form of limited, regular self-assessment, whether during their own breaks, lunchtime, or even while sitting in their cubicles with their eyes closed for a few minutes. Self-assessment is simply the process of evaluating yourself based on a standard of competencies or a set of goals, and most employees often think about the work they've done in some capacity. These assessments involve evaluating their performance and identifying areas for improvement. I have spoken with many employees who express a desire to excel in their job, be valuable to the company, and receive appropriate recognition and rewards.

However, some employees may struggle with asking for help for fear it may be perceived as a sign of weakness or lack of knowledge. It is important for managers to understand and support "all" employees in this regard and provide opportunities for growth and advancement.

One way to foster an environment of growth and development is by allowing employees to have regular "moments of silence" during which they can reflect on their performance, reassess their situation, and consider the various factors impacting their work. This self-evaluation process is vital for employees who may often feel isolated and unsupported in their roles, as if they are stranded on an island without the necessary resources to succeed.

To address this, employers should provide employees with the necessary support and resources to help them navigate their roles and achieve success. This can include providing them with communication channels to connect with others, as well as the tools and resources they need to perform their job effectively. These resources can be thought of as bridges to connect the employee to the necessary support and resources and as carrier pigeons that allow for communication and connection with others. The necessary tools and resources will help them to thrive in their role. These efforts are crucial in creating a supportive environment for employees and ensuring their success.

Examination and reassessment are important parts of the process that both employees and managers must go through to ensure a company is operating efficiently. It involves constantly evaluating the current situation in the department and making adjustments as necessary. If a manager determines a department is overstaffed, they should speak with key supervisors to identify areas where staff could be reduced or positions could be changed to part-time. This process is ongoing and requires constant reevaluation to ensure the company is on the right track. However, it is important for management to involve the employees in the process and communicate their decisions, as a lack of transparency can lead to mistrust and a lack of employee engagement. A positive company culture, built through involvement and communication, is key to ensuring employees are happy and productive.

THOUGHT MANAGEMENT

- In your past experience, how have you blended the missions of management, the company, and the employee successfully to accomplish your goals? What did you learn in the process?

- What are some of the biggest challenges you have experienced when outlining your mission?

- As your mission evolves, how can you communicate its evolution to the various levels within your organization?

CHAPTER 6

SELF-ASSESSMENT & DEVELOPMENT PLANS

"To be aware of a single shortcoming in oneself is more useful than to be aware of a thousand in someone else."

DALAI LAMA

When it comes to assessing how employees act in a team setting, there are several types of assessments available. Among the most popular are Myers Briggs and DISC, but there are many more as well. These measure a variety of personal traits and can help teams identify areas of improvement as well as individual strengths and weaknesses. Other popular forms of testing include the Stanford-Binet test, which focuses on cognitive abilities, and the Wechsler Adult Intelligence Score, which is used to judge intelligence levels. With so many emotional and behavioral tests available, it's never been easier to develop and promote an effective team environment to ensure peak performance among its members.

However, despite their usefulness, these tests tend to focus on outcomes and may not fully consider the human element involved in assessment and decision-making. To be successful in achieving desired results, it is important to intimately understand the situation and the staff you are working with. Without this knowledge, all the testing and assessment can do is provide projections that miss crucial insights and context into the problem at hand. Ultimately, the best approach is to bridge testing with human experience and rely on both sides of that equation for better understanding.

Reassessment is an important part of any project, great or small. Whether you are looking at evaluating employees, gauging performance, or measuring the cost-effectiveness of a product, it is important to take a step back and ensure the elements and principles involved are still valid. The reassessment process allows you to verify what you have worked hard to accomplish actually aligns with the intended objectives. It ensures the final results can actually provide a strong foundation for whatever project you are working on. By taking the time to reassess your project after a certain point, you can be sure your efforts will yield positive results in the future.

It's a mistake to do something once and expect the same outcome in the future. Nothing remains the same from one day to another, and dynamic changes affect everything, including businesses, so reevaluation needs to be an ongoing process if individuals want their endeavors to succeed. Failing to recognize this could lead someone down a path of failure because they are missing the bigger picture. Everything needs to be constantly reappraised, so you'll need to look at the complete situation and take into consideration all variables in order to achieve success. It is also important for teams to recognize individuals are going through changes every day, which means elements are viewed from different perspectives from person to person and day to day. If a business pays attention to each aspect as part of the holistic picture, then success can and should be achieved. However, a lack of reevaluation can result in failure.

THE SCOPE OF SELF-ASSESSMENT

Self-assessment in a company is of the utmost importance, as it helps organizations identify their strengths and weaknesses. You need to consider absolutely everything, from the team you have assembled to the resources available, and each unique situation encountered. An effective assessment will ensure management is able to use each of these components properly or a combination of them all. Accounting for different factors like organizational processes, customer service, products, services, and leadership are all paramount for having a successful business. Though it can be a daunting task to review each one of these elements thoroughly, careful consideration, understanding, and interpretation of them can optimize any organization's outcomes and decisions can be made to help create an even stronger foundation for the company. Doing this can significantly improve the performance of any organization.

Before starting any major business project, it is important to have a plan in place. The first step to reaching a goal, such as creating 12,000 widgets in a year, is hiring personnel who can fulfill the required output. After staffing has been set, strategic processes and plans should be created to outline what materials, resources, and assessments are necessary to build the widgets. Along with this, employees with the appropriate abilities need to be put in place to oversee the production and organization of widgets to ensure they reach their goal of 1,000 each month. This process also allows for room to modify any assigned processes as needed or change them up as you move forward and grow your KPIs for success. Utilizing assessments before moving forward guarantees the best possible outcome for each project or aspect within your organization.

STAGES OF SELF-ASSESSMENT

Self-assessment is an important process for organizations to ensure they are on the right track. There are three processes in particular that help them with this: examine, reassess, and reexamine.

Examine

During the examination phase of corporate decision-making, it is essential for companies to take a critical look at existing policies and procedures. This often requires careful and thoughtful internal review. In some cases, external experts on process, products, distribution, and sales can provide valuable insight to supplement the process. Consulting firms can bring fresh perspectives, offer useful recommendations based on their extensive industry expertise, and save time by allowing executives to focus on more pressing matters. If organizations feel outside sources could help them make more well-informed changes, then they should seriously consider doing it.

Reassess

After collecting and analyzing key performance indicators, it's time for an organization to reassess its strategies for self-assessment and development. This often requires stakeholders to go back to the drawing board and make any necessary changes or improvements based on the results of the assessment phase. A thorough review helps ensure all goals are still valid and that any new trends or insights have been accounted for. Self-assessment is a powerful tool and should not be taken lightly. Careful consideration of the process of reassessment should result in beneficial outcomes for the organization. Covering this again here may seem redundant, but reassessment is such an important part of the process, so the redundancy is not only warranted but necessary.

Reexamine

Finally, these changes should be reexamined periodically to ensure they still align with the goals of the organization. Ongoing reviews allow organizations to identify areas in which they are exceeding expectations, as well as potential areas or projects where modifications or additional resources may be required. Regularly reexamining organizational objectives and progress can also provide insight into potential shifts that should be made over time with respect to the collective goals of the business.

An organization's ability to assess its activities and modify operations accordingly is an essential factor in achieving long-term success. Self-assessment is a valuable tool for organizations wanting to stay competitive in today's market, and these three processes can help them achieve that goal.

THE IMPORTANCE OF THE HUMAN ELEMENT

All too often, work becomes a series of hourly shifts and delivering expected outputs rather than striving for specific goals. This is a major challenge for businesses today. Shifting this mindset requires pushing employees and supervisors out of their comfort zone, encouraging them to think beyond meeting their quota, and allowing them to explore ways to reach milestones, even if they are not typically assigned as objectives. Encouraging this type of behavior helps direct employees to focus on results rather than on time spent at work, ultimately benefiting the business. To nudge employees towards this goal-oriented mentality, it's important to provide accessible resources such as training sessions and discussions about goal setting for those in leadership roles. Additionally, holding regular check-ins with staff can be a helpful tool for providing support when it comes to reaching individual objectives, whether small or large.

Adding this human element into an organization's planning and assessment is critical for success. Doing so requires more than just implementing processes; it's about caring for and connecting with your employees. Companies must be willing to invest in a culture of unity, understanding, and active listening to identify what employees are working on, how they're handling it, and what can be done to help them reach the finish line faster. Assessing the goals set by the company against real-world results is necessary to make sure progress is being made efficiently. This cycle of assessment, implementation, and reassessment should continue until optimal results are achieved. Through this approach, organizations can try to ensure everyone involved has the opportunity to be seen and heard, which leads to greater productivity and improved morale.

KEY ELEMENTS OF SELF-ASSESSMENT

Self-assessment is a powerful tool for both individual and organizational betterment. Used properly, the same general process of self-assessment can be used across an organization regardless of who or what is being assessed. By guiding each individual and team to thoughtfully evaluate their strengths, weaknesses, and areas of improvement, organizations can inspire meaningful engagement as well as measure and track progress toward defined goals. It requires cultivating open dialogue and honest reflection while providing feedback designed to promote growth. If done correctly, it has the potential to lead to higher-level performance across a wide range of endeavors. The trick is to understand your team's needs well enough so you can design the best possible approach for implementing self-assessment processes. Get creative in your designs, so the practice feels tailored to their occupational environment and brings value beyond a score or a criterion. Here are the four processes of self-assessment.

Intention

When conducting a self-assessment of your organization, the first thing to take into consideration is whether you achieved your initial mission statement or goal. It is important to accurately assess what you have and have not accomplished. Taking an honest bird's-eye view of the situation can provide valuable insight into where changes need to be made or what successes can be celebrated moving forward. A thorough review of your success and failures in relation to the original purpose and intention of the organization serves as a foundation for continued growth.

Buy-in

One of the most important parts of this process is gauging the reaction from your employees. Did they buy in when you explained your goals? If so, how did that affect the team dynamic? A positive response indicates unity and commitment to the goal and sets a marker for how effective the future development of the organization can and will be. Seeing if employees responded positively helps measure if your mission is clear and how well it resonated. By making sure you're connected to those around you, you can implement more successful changes and gauge progress accordingly.

Improvements

When assessing your organization, it's necessary to consider whether or not your employees truly adopted your idea and worked to improve the company. This requires listening to the feedback from your team and taking action on ways to further improve buy-in. A key indicator of success is when the employees of your organization come together on a single vision and show loyalty to its implementation. If the engagement of your team is high, then you can be more confident that the changes are sustainable and it would be worthwhile to further invest in development. On the other side, if morale has been low and there has been frequent pushback against new initiatives, then reassessing what can be done differently is highly advised. Engaging with members to get their feedback and ideas should always be central to any efforts toward improving organizational performance.

Requirements Met

When it comes to self-assessment, the focus should be on ensuring the required results have been achieved once all employees have bought into the program. This allows organizations to look objectively at their performance – what went well and what could be improved upon. A comprehensive review includes the key contributions of each employee, enabling them to reflect and provide feedback on their success so further progress can be made across the entire organization. Self-assessments offer valuable insight into how things are being handled and also provide an opportunity for employees to have their voices heard. Ultimately, this can help create a more transparent workplace culture and lead to greater improvements in productivity and efficiency.

This self-assessment process takes practice to master. When taken seriously and implemented in a regular way, it can become second nature. Your mind will already be running through the first two steps of the process before you even realize what's going on, and you'll feel ready and prepared to move on to step three. It's all about trusting yourself and your thought processes while acknowledging them as valuable guides for finding clarity and direction.

In one of my previous jobs, I was responsible for domestic and non-domestic outsourcing. This included both finding employees within the United States, Canada, or Mexico and sources from foreign countries such as India, Vietnam, Indonesia, China, and Costa Rica to name a few. At that time, the words "Made in America" resonated with me, so I saw the strength of our industry and the hardworking American people. Many leaders and managers had their opinions as outsourcing of both manufacturing and call centers to other countries increased, and challenges in training, urgency, and communications began to arise.

Solving these challenges required a "We can do this!" mentality. This was depicted in a World War II poster of Rosie the Riveter, which represented just how resilient American workers were, even in periods of turmoil and uncertainty. I understood the "We" in "We can do it!" meant I also had to get extensive consultation or input from my team. If these feelings affected my opinion on whether we should outsource domestically or non-domestically, they were bound to affect the views of my team as well. I knew I couldn't make such a big decision without any extensive consultation or input from my team.

So, I decided to incorporate the human element into this decision-making and took my managers to places where we previously outsourced our work, both domestic and non-domestic locations. Visiting these locations was an eye-opening experience and gave my management team the best view of our options. In the Philippines, Costa Rica, and India, we toured the factories and spoke with those in charge to get an even deeper understanding of what was available in terms of processes and products. We asked questions about their approach, how to handle our requests, improvements they made that could benefit us, and details on other clients when available and applicable. Sure enough, after doing first-hand observations and research, we were able to make a well-informed opinion about our outsourcing needs.

Upon completion of the trip, attention was given to how well the outsourcers performed in various processes including lien releases on mortgage loans, making tax payments, building welcome packages, processing paperwork, and handling a call center. After a thorough study and a comprehensive report, it was determined that the lack of experience and low level of expertise made the outsourcers unable to work on tasks like lien releases or call centers. However, they showed aptitude and potential when presented with activities such as local taxes or building welcome packages.

We then visited domestic outsourcers, and one factor made the decision relatively simple – most of the positions had already been filled by experienced mortgage bankers. Working as an outsourcer, instead of a mortgage banker, made it easier for employees to talk to customers on the phone and handle other important processes with greater speed and accuracy. Domestic outsourcers also had the necessary experience to handle phone calls from customers, and their familiarity with native English lent itself brilliantly to effective communication. Additionally, they were able to understand and handle tasks such as processing paperwork or building welcome packages and lien releases because they had experience working with these tasks before.

Then, calculations needed to be done for assessment purposes, which required hiring a workforce with a specialized, high-level education to do this job. In India, the workforce at outsourcing companies typically had bachelor's degrees and a large amount of knowledge in technical work. However, when it came to outsourcing in the United States, these same higher-level educational requirements were not always met. This discrepancy can often lead to different levels of productivity, with Indian outsourcing offering a better-educated staff and more reliable results, so we had to consider the educational background as a relative part of our decision criteria.

The only aspect left was the cost, which is always important in decision-making. Outsourcing is often seen as a cost-saving measure for companies looking to reduce their overhead expenses. An accounting specialist was able to provide insight by running the analytics on it, and the results revealed outsourcing non-domestically could lead to substantial savings. Though the outsourcers and U.S. companies charged roughly the same amount, the outsourcers paid their employees substantially less per hour and did not pay their employees' benefits. However, U.S. companies paid their in-house employees more and contributed to their benefits, so more of that money went to the employees than the company itself. While this was a comparison with in-house employees, there was still no denying that outsourcing non-domestically was the much cheaper option.

While outsourcing work to other countries often appears to be a more cost-effective solution than using domestic labor, there are many hidden costs associated with this decision that could undermine potential savings such as cultural and communication problems as well as insufficient training and unfamiliarity with the tasks at hand. In many cases, these additional costs may be difficult to anticipate or predict, risking bad public relations for the company and leading to an even bigger financial loss in the end. As such, we had to carefully consider all aspects before making a final decision when it came to outsourcing work abroad.

Any time you make changes or decide to go in a new direction, you have to assess and evaluate different elements to determine whether or not the method is working as it should be. It's important to understand what employees are expected to know before making assumptions and expecting them to get the job done. Factors like pricing and potential hidden fees must be taken into account; otherwise, it can cause problems further down the line. Suggestions for improvement should be actively given during the test phase, and they should only be fully implemented once the improvement proves to be effective in avoiding any costly mistakes.

Completing assessments, evaluations, and processes can be a difficult task, but they ultimately provide excellent insight into where you wish to end up. At the end of the day, it is important to accurately review all your work and ensure each step has been taken to reach the desired outcome. Taking the time to study the process is beneficial and will be reflected when you start implementing your ideas in real-world applications.

OPEN-MINDEDNESS

When it comes to assessment and evaluation in an organization, striking a balance can be difficult. It's important to stay open-minded, able to adjust and accommodate new ideas, but being too flexible could actually prevent progress in an organization. The trick is knowing the right time to try something new and understanding when your team has moved too far off the topic of what you have set out to achieve. There is always a risk in not maintaining focus, and making sure to keep an eye on what the end goal is while also allowing creativity and innovation are critical considerations when assessing or evaluating any situation. Finding this middle ground requires careful thought and consideration to make decisions and have clear objectives in mind beforehand.

Trying to institute change in the workplace can be difficult, and sometimes when a new leader arrives, there is an assumption their methods have been successful before and, therefore, must be successful this time. This could lead them to decision-making without properly assessing whether those changes are necessary or appropriate for your organization. They may come in with an ego so big they believe they already know best and try to immediately start implementing changes solely based on what has worked for them in the past. But this approach doesn't always work because conditions vary from company to company, which is why you will need to thoroughly assess if any changes are needed, no matter how experienced the incoming leader is or is believed to be.

When implementing new strategies or protocols, the structure's setup should be realistic enough for the team to have a high probability of success while also not asking them to do too much at once, so they aren't overwhelmed by the process. Although it may be tempting to assume the methods used by this leader previously will yield similar results, you will need to remain open-minded and flexible when entrusting someone with a new position. It is impossible to account for all of the moving pieces at play in any given situation, so successful adaptation and evolution to changing conditions are key. Trying to undertake too many changes or make demands that are too challenging can often lead to small failures, which, if not addressed in a timely manner, could eventually cause a large-scale failure of the overall process.

A common problem seen in larger companies is the tendency to bring in "hired guns" from outside the company, who they think can magically fix everything. Even if they do manage to patch up a problem, there is a high probability of them making it worse before it gets any better. This usually stems from giving directions that make employees feel like their process-based work or contribution isn't valued as much as before, which can be damaging to the business structure and creates a hostile environment where information cannot be easily shared with colleagues. Embracing and involving all members of the team, both internal and external, is key to successful management in any company, which is why we need to be open-minded – but not so open-minded that we sacrifice the human element of the staff on the front lines of our companies.

THE POWER OF CONVERSATION

Management by walking around has always been an important tool for me. After all, the best way to understand the intricacies of any company and its individual employees is to talk to each of them directly in their workspaces. I actively engage with them by asking about their job roles, what areas they feel confident in, and where they think I might be able to help. Doing this helps me get to know each of my employees on a deeper level and enables me to better serve their needs. As a result, there is greater efficiency within our overall team, and each employee feels valued.

Questioning my team members on task-related matters is one of my favorite things to do because it gives me an opportunity to learn the ins and outs of how a certain job is done, which can inform my individual skill set as well as the collective skill set of my team. I'm also able to make connections with staff members who I may not have otherwise. Perpetually asking questions allows me to gain perspective from a variety of employees, ensures I have an understanding of the different departments within an organization, and keeps me in tune with what's happening around me. The best part is these questions do not necessarily have to be related to any specific skill or assignment.

Here are a few questions you can try asking:

- What's the easiest thing about your job?
- What's the hardest thing about your job?
- What can we do to help you do your job better?
- How can we help you create a more quality product or perform better?

Developing a sense of connection with the employees around us and being confident in having conversations, rather than just providing orders or directives, is essential to leadership. While some team members may be reluctant to engage in dialogue, creating productive relationships with team members can be the foundation for organizational success.

I once had the pleasure of meeting an incredibly helpful salesman at a clothing shop that sold large men's clothing. As a person who wears XXL-sized clothes, this was a store that aligned with my needs. I was intrigued by how trim the salesman was – almost too slim for the job! It didn't make sense what a slim guy like him was doing working in a store like this. When I asked him why he pursued this line of work instead of something more traditionally suitable to his body type, he simply stated he always wanted to assist humankind by helping men find clothing that actually fit them properly, which is rather difficult in most traditional stores. It was clear this man genuinely wanted to make sure all men looked as good in their clothing as he did in his – mission accomplished!

This applies to management as well. Managing a successful business requires more than just coming up with well-thought-out plans. It also requires considering the opinions of your team and actively working together to create something bigger than yourself. When we think about our employees' input, caring for their needs, and encouraging their participation in decision-making throughout the organization, we are better positioned to be successful in our strategies. Good management goes hand-in-hand with assessing and reworking processes as needed, and we can only understand what works and what doesn't through a constant feedback loop. Having the right employees on board and taking their input into consideration when appropriate will make all the difference in your organization, but all of this requires you to have meaningful conversations with your staff at all levels.

SELF-ASSESSMENT VS. DEVELOPMENT PLAN

Self-assessment and development plans can both be powerful tools for personal growth. Self-assessment is the process of evaluating yourself based on a standard of competencies or a set of goals. It can help identify tendencies or areas that need improvement so employees can work toward them. On the other hand, development plans are like a map to get where you want to go. They help you make decisions on investments of time and resources while also focusing on what makes the most sense.

Self-assessment is a necessary evil and needs to be done constantly to ensure you stay on track with what you're planning to accomplish or working toward. Too often, we allow our ego to get in the way and think we know how to do everything or that the way we do something is better than how anybody else would do it. This type of mentality will prevent you from achieving anything. This is why you need to put your ego to the side and constantly self-assess. The self-assessment involves yourself (obviously) but also how you interact with people around you to accomplish a goal. It's not something that you can sit down and do for five minutes, then say it's done. It needs to be done constantly and continuously.

If you do the appropriate self-assessment, you can create a roadmap for yourself of all the different areas you need to work on on a daily basis to continue to develop yourself as you move along. By doing this, you continue to stay on top of your self-development in the process. In other words, self-development happens as a result of good self-assessment.

The better you get at self-assessment and self-development, the better manager you will become. You will start to correct your own behaviors, have better conversations with your team, and be open to new solutions. Because of this deep understanding of yourself, the job, and what your employees are going through, you can give proper guidance to your employees and help them with their own development process. Employees are a business's greatest asset, and to waste that asset is terrible. The only way to fully utilize this asset is to engage with people, listen to what they're saying, interpret your understanding of it, then react to it through self-assessment so you can make better decisions in the future that align with your overall mission. With both processes, it's important to remain self-aware and be honest but constructive in how you analyze your actions and outcomes.

Self-assessment and development plans should not be considered separately. You should think of one leading to another, and they should ultimately meld together into something larger. It is important to take both into consideration to properly determine areas of strength and weaknesses so an individual can continue on a path of growth and improvement. Because self-assessment and development plans are intertwined, it is essential to view them holistically in order to best assess one's abilities.

MANAGING FINANCES WHEN EXPLORING OPTIONS

Exploring different options in your business can be a daunting process, so you will need to manage your finances well during this time by keeping track of your spending. This means setting a budget, avoiding unnecessary purchases, and maintaining organized records of how much you're spending and on what. Exploring options doesn't always have to break the bank though. Taking advantage of resources like free budgeting software or helpful articles from finance experts can make the entire process much more manageable. With responsible financial privacy and sensible goal setting, you can go forth with peace of mind knowing you are securely managing your funds.

There are three ways you can explore your options without wasting valuable resources such as time, energy, effort, and money:

Do Your Research

Companies are increasingly doing their research to save time and money in the long run. They take the time to explore what services are offered and compare prices across multiple industries. This allows them to receive accurate cost estimates before committing to a service. As a result, more and more companies are reaching out to others with similar needs for guidance on how they successfully completed their project without breaking the bank. By taking a comprehensive approach like this, businesses can be sure they're making an informed decision that will provide the most value in the long run.

The Human Element

As a business, understanding how the potential consequences of your decisions can impact your team is essential, so you need to make sure everyone involved gets the most out of any situation. This means bringing the human element into the decision-making process and understanding the exact effects it could have on your team. Management must also think about how customers will react to their decisions because they may have implications on whether customers feel like they can trust them or not. All of these considerations must go through a process and be "run up the flagpole" so all decisions can be made responsibly.

The Community

It is important to consider the broader community when making decisions. Connecting with local professionals and networks can lead to business opportunities that may not have been attainable without their help. Supporting businesses within the community will help you gain greater insight into what types of options are available and offer incentives for customers or employees who live nearby. It's important to recognize the value of engaging with local resources and understanding how they can impact financial decisions within the company. Doing so can increase visibility, foster relationships, and amplify growth in ways other methods may not be able to accomplish.

A great example of putting the value of community into practice is found in a mortgage banking outsourcing company based in Oklahoma. The company was founded by a mortgage banking professional of American Indian heritage, and he chose to employ individuals primarily from an Indian reservation who have had limited opportunities but who were trainable, talented, and eager for opportunity. They developed their skills further through an intensive training program. The result has been impressive, as they now produce quality work while earning higher salaries than they ever previously had the opportunity to. This instance of prioritizing external development over individual interest leads to greater success for the company, community, and its employees alike.

Companies have to weigh the investment they can make in their own culture and communities more broadly. This is especially important in communities with fewer opportunities and limited access to resources that could help employees excel. For example, the business leader mentioned above recently highlighted opportunities to invest in the rural Oklahoma population, which was hugely appealing for those who wanted to stay and make something of their lives there. Before this, these individuals had not had the opportunity to succeed professionally in the work environment. Thanks to this investment, these employees are now becoming superstars in their local community.

THOUGHT MANAGEMENT

- What practices do you use to self-assess and how often do you perform self-assessments?
- How can you use self-assessment to create development plans for yourself and your team?
- How often do you engage in conversation with your employees on the front lines outside of formal meetings? How can you make a better effort to do that in your daily or weekly efforts?

CHAPTER 7

MAKING YOURSELF REQUIRED

"The only indispensable people are those who take joy
in their work and who do it with such vigor that they
infect others with their enthusiasm."

CHARLES DE GAULLE

Making yourself required means making yourself indispensable. A good manager or employee is going to keep their ears open and learn what's happening in the environment around them, whether it's in their own department, a department they interface with, or coming directly from their boss. When you hear the expectations being set and the issues being discussed, you have the opportunity to give feedback and insights. When it doesn't necessarily fall within the areas you are responsible for and it's unexpected, you make yourself required because you are giving proactive feedback to a situation you know about. You may not know every element, but you can give them a unique perspective from your experience, which shows you care about the company and what they are trying to achieve.

As a manager, we have to be open-minded to those employees who share genuine insights to help us achieve our goals quicker, better, and faster because they allow us to solve current and future problems. They may not be an expert, but they have likely observed what is happening on the ground and can give unique feedback that is indispensable to the success of the department or company.

When we are open-minded and accept input from others, we can respond to the issues we are dealing with more effectively. That's why consulting with someone and asking for their opinion is a crucial step to take before heading down a specific path. These conversations allow individuals to use the insights they have gained from life experience to make informed decisions.

COLLABORATIVE MEETINGS

I firmly believe in having weekly management meetings as a key part of my workload. Since I value the effective use of an individual's time, these meetings are always kept to no more than an hour, with a minimum duration typically around 30 minutes. Naturally, this can be difficult for some individuals who prefer longer conversations, yet it helps encourage our team to stay focused on the issues at hand and get back to their tasks promptly. Not only does this benefit them by not cutting into their daily productivity, but it also allows us to maintain a clear structure in our meetings so everyone has the opportunity to speak up and express themselves while staying efficient.

Whenever I walk into a meeting where no one is talking, I know something's wrong. By instilling open dialogue in your company culture, you can avoid this and everyone will feel more comfortable sharing. I always start each meeting by having a quick report about what our department is working on to give some context. Then, I'll ask everyone in the room to share three extra observations or recommendations related to the information we just discussed or shared and how it relates to their work. This simple step engages participants and keeps conversations flowing.

As long as you appropriately moderate the meeting, this exercise only takes about fifteen minutes out of an hour-long meeting with eight or nine employees present. Remember, your job as a leader is to lead meetings by striking the balance between encouraging staff to speak their minds and moderating to keep everyone on track. Though it isn't required for every meeting, this method has helped our group stay organized while also connecting in an informal way.

During my weekly management meetings, I always ask each department's management personnel present to share their current successes, challenges, opportunities, and concerns. Additionally, I prompt them to reflect over the last week and consider what their biggest obstacle was and how they overcame it, if at all. In one meeting, one of the managers mentioned their greatest challenge was attempting to cram two weeks' worth of tasks into a single week. Being able to relate to this struggle, I then asked them what measures they took to resolve the problem. It is always interesting to hear the solutions managers come up with and see which strategies have been successful and which haven't been as effective.

After gathering my employees together and outlining the tasks that need to be accomplished, I delegate different responsibilities to individuals. Then, I have them come back together and consolidate their efforts into a viable plan. We all work together to fine-tune the details and make sure everyone is on board. After listening carefully to various perspectives, we agree upon an actionable strategy and begin implementation.

With a team plan clearly laid out in front of us, I am always filled with admiration for the initiative my employees have taken to make it happen. In an effort to maximize efficiency, everyone works together as a unit, ensuring every piece of the puzzle fits together perfectly. With difficult tasks ahead, we plan accordingly by supporting each other's ideas and feedback while eliminating any possibility of errors or miscommunication. This combination of collaboration and analytics is key in helping devise a plan to efficiently and effectively reach our goals.

Drawing on the experience of my career, I have recognized that calling in other staff members to help solve a problem creates an opportunity for collaboration. Initially, they are often surprised when they are asked to help, but the surprise is quickly replaced by enthusiasm when they understand they have an important role in coming up with a resolution. By giving employees responsibility, their engagement increases, and they will be more likely to contribute their ideas. It is also beneficial to invite support from those around them and stress how no one needs to tackle any challenge alone.

Their input can be invaluable in finding the right solution and working together towards the same goal.

When you ask your employees for help and advice, it can be a win-win situation for both the organization and the individuals involved. Not only does it foster a sense of self-esteem and respect within the department – after all, you are demonstrating that their opinions matter – but it also ensures greater understanding and knowledge within the groups and that any decisions made are based on sound information and sources. Plus, you are consulting those with the actual expertise, so they won't be surprised when implementation begins. Asking your other employees for help and advice can help foster collaborative efforts and collective awareness of your goals, aspirations, and problem-solving abilities for the company.

COMMUNICATION

Communication is key to making sure your organization understands the value you bring to the workplace. Effective communication allows you to express yourself clearly, demonstrate the skills and knowledge you have, and show how you can be a great asset to the team. When communicating, stay professional and conscious of who your audience is and pitch ideas in ways that appeal to those who will receive them. Whether it's through email updates, coordinating virtual meetings, or even scheduling quick face-to-face chats with everyone on your team, proper communication strategies can help strengthen relationships and prove your worth in any organization.

Finding the right balance of assertiveness, politeness, and organization is crucial to be recognized as a leader in your workplace. One of the best ways to gain respect from colleagues and superiors is by showing your willingness to be open to suggestions and take responsibility for mistakes. Allowing questions from those around you creates a culture of collaboration and lets everyone know their impact on the task at hand matters. Pay attention to the verbal discussion as well as the nonverbal cues, such as body language and eye contact, because they can make a huge difference in how employees perceive communication. Lastly, be sure to be on time when setting meetings or making presentations. It shows you take your responsibility seriously and can effectively manage tasks without having stressful consequences. Communicating successfully with respect and reliability will make employees feel comfortable following your lead.

Here are some ways in which you can make yourself required through effective communication at work:

Be Respectful

As a team leader, it's important to stay mindful of the impact your words have on those you work with. Respectfully communicating with your team allows for healthy relationships to develop and makes everyone feel their opinion is valued. It also ensures everyone's dignity is preserved when disagreements can be had without contention or an escalation in emotions. This way, tasks can still get completed and goals can be met without any damage being done to relationships between team members. Mutual respect is key to forming strong working relationships conducive to learning and collaboration.

Give Clear Feedback

As a leader, the ability to provide both obvious and precise input and feedback about the tasks at hand is absolutely essential for making sure everyone involved in a project or group can succeed. Clear instructions and constructive critiques are truly the backbones of any good team. Feedback should also be timely and consistent to help keep everyone on track with their goals. Making sure appropriate input is given allows teammates or coworkers to reach their desired outcome with a shared understanding of what should be done.

Set Expectations

Setting expectations for communication is two-fold: you need to establish expectations *for* communication and establish expectations *through* communication. Establishing expectations *for* communication is essential because everyone has a preferred method for how they speak to others and are spoken to. Although the method of communication via email, phone, or in person is important, it's also about the tone, context, and environment for communication. Set expectations about how you want to be communicated with as a leader and find out how each team member likes to be communicated with.

You should also establish expectations *through* communication. Clear communication of the goals and objectives everyone has to meet enables all participants to have a clear understanding of what is expected from them. This can help you set a plan for working together to reach those goals and avoid any potential issues down the road. By having a common frame of reference for their mission, everyone involved will be able to work together more effectively, making it easier and faster to accomplish the goal at hand. With clarity of expectations, progress will be noticed more quickly, and motivation will be kept high among all team members involved in the project.

Ask Questions

Asking questions can be an incredibly effective way to gain insight into the progress and challenges each of your team members is facing. Not only does it give you a better understanding of their efforts and successes, but it also helps build relationships, trust, and communication within the team. It's important to ask questions openly and without judgment to encourage honest dialogue and determine what strategies may be beneficial for improvement. Keep in mind not all issues will surface merely through conversations, so gathering feedback through surveys or comment boxes can provide even more detailed information about how tasks are being handled by team members. All in all, asking plenty of questions ensures you have an accurate view of what's happening on your team.

Listen Actively

Active listening is an important skill for any leader to have. It is not just about hearing what other individuals are saying, but it also involves reading between the lines and understanding the individual's needs and feelings. This involves consciously focusing on what the speaker's body language is displaying and taking their feelings into account along with the words.

Thinking in a box is commonly used in management to describe people who lack communication skills, which prevents them from solving real-world problems. These people are usually either new to management or have been in a management position for a long time but were never trained properly to manage others. Thinking in a box can be detrimental to a company, so it's important to recognize this early on and provide development for these managers to encourage them to think more outside of the box. We usually offer specialized training to these managers to help pull them out of their shells.

The most effective leaders are the ones who communicate back and forth with the employees they manage, the people who manage them, and the customers they are serving. Effective leaders are able to communicate with empathy, openness, and respect on all management levels, which is key to fostering a collaborative work environment. Being an active listener will help enhance relationships between coworkers and motivate employees to achieve maximum productivity for both the organization and its leader.

Effective communication between the leader and the team is paramount to a successful team and organization. In a business setting, having project managers who are willing to communicate effectively can make all the difference in a project's success. The manager must strive to make sure all their team members have a thorough grasp of the scope of a project. They can do this by providing detailed notes and showing them various examples of what the finished project should look like. It is also important to create an environment where employees can ask questions without fear of not being heard or understood. Unfortunately, not every manager strikes the appropriate balance in their approach, which can leave employees feeling baffled instead of enlightened.

Leaders should strive to provide two-way communication whenever possible. Making statements like "What did you mean, John?" or "John, is this what I heard you say?" are actually signs of strength, not weakness. When leaders do this, they show they care enough to give their team the right information while also giving them a chance to clarify their idea if it wasn't understood correctly. On the other hand, offering an answer or solution without giving a team member a chance to ask any follow-up questions can be problematic as they may end up receiving incorrect information. While employees may understand this as an important practice in an educational setting, they fail to realize that the same goes for the workplace.

SELLABLE

Everyone knows communication is fundamental for humans – it is a means of expressing needs, feelings, and ideas. But without the intention of making something sellable and attractive to the audience, communication can quickly become meaningless. Effective communication is essential to getting ahead in the workplace and a critical component of this is the ability to effectively sell your idea. Whether it's pitching a new project or making an argument in a meeting, successful communicators know how to capture their audience's attention and make their points in an interesting and persuasive way. Being able to articulate your thoughts well is only one part of communication though. You must also be able to put your ideas into words your team members can understand and convince them of your point.

This is not to say communication can't be meaningful without driving sales or influencing behavior, but if there is no intention of action, more often than not, your words will just get lost in the noise. In order for your message to stand out from all the chatter and create an impactful connection, you must ensure you are creating content that's irresistible – that outshines, entices, and engages all those who interact with it. To make communication useful, it should add value, be relevant, and have an underlying intent to draw staff members in. Communication is an art form, one which requires both confidence and eloquence. With practice, anyone can learn the key to communication and confidently sell their ideas.

A good example of this is the communication we receive from news outlets. During hurricanes, blizzards, and other harsh weather conditions, the meteorologist on the news generally warns those in the area not to go outside or drive due to safety reasons. Cars can break down, travelers can go missing, and it can be difficult for rescue teams to help. Even with such dire warnings, people continue to go out, which is a testament to how difficult it can be for communicators to deliver and sell a message. For a message to be effective, it must be presented in a way that inspires people to take action without having to be explicitly asked.

The power of effective communication to sell a message can be demonstrated when two hours later, the same newscaster repeats his report about a local incident and includes the photographs of cars that had skidded off the road, an ambulance with emergency lights flashing, and other salient media. These images spur viewers to pay attention to the story. Only then do the viewers begin to believe what they previously refused to acknowledge. This illustrates the importance of not only communicating information but also presenting it in an engaging way capable of selling the reported story. It was the same message, but now, it was presented in a more sellable manner. In this case, the combination of words and visuals created the necessary impact to demonstrate to viewers what they were seeing was real and pressing.

Just like this TV reporter, being sellable is an important part of any job and plays a big role in preventing people from getting hurt on the job. It is essential to find the balance between causing people to be over-cautious and fearful of risks, yet also accurately outlining dangers and hazards. Being too careful can be just as dangerous as being oblivious to the situation because one may miss signals of actual danger. It's important to provide guidance for people to function at their desired level of safety and comfort while still handling tasks correctly and effectively.

Understanding what level of sellable communication to use and who you are speaking with is key when trying to convey confidence, conviction, and passion in a certain message. Depending on who you are engaging with, the way you present your idea may have to be adjusted. If the person is easily persuaded, all you have to do is explain what needs to be done. But when dealing with someone more skeptical, presenting more evidence or providing a strong rationale would be necessary. Lastly, if you really need to motivate someone to take action, you can elaborate more on the plan by describing plausible benefits or reward possibilities that might come from performing this task.

FOUR PILLARS OF SELLABLE COMMUNICATION

Clearly communicating your ideas to your employees is essential for effective teamwork and productivity. You can use these four pillars to focus your communication on sellability.

Think It Through

Before attempting to communicate your concepts, think through what the ideal outcome would be and develop the best way to convey that goal. Once this is determined, take an extra moment to make sure everyone understands the objectives thoroughly and all of the particulars are taken into account. By taking these steps, you can ensure your message will be shared concisely with your team in a sellable manner.

Employee Buy-in

When thinking about great communication, one of the goals should be to make sure everyone is buying in. Strong relationships with employees built on trust and respect are key, so it's important to think beyond providing directives or job expectations. If you want successful communication with your employees, try engaging them in conversation, listening to their ideas and concerns, recognizing their contributions, and having empathy. This level of connection will work wonders toward increasing employee engagement and productivity.

Assurance

If employers want to ensure successful outcomes from their employees' endeavors and want them to enthusiastically work on the tasks they are assigned, they need to provide assurance that their effort will be met with results. Reaching mutually fulfilling goals between the employer and employee will produce greater productivity and improved workplace morale. By distilling this message to each employee through clear, productive communication, you can ensure a profitable outcome while maintaining workplace satisfaction.

Personal Examples

One way to incorporate sellable communication is by creating an emotional connection, rather than just providing a list of facts and figures. To effectively communicate with your employees, be open about your personal experiences related to the topic. Sharing relevant stories helps establish a bond with them, leading to more collaborative conversations, which can increase productivity and help with problem-solving. Ultimately, by conveying your point through personal examples, you will build stronger relationships and improve both understanding and engagement with your team.

Hearing positive feedback from my employees always fills me with pride and joy. Some of the best moments are when an employee comes up to me and tells me they understand something after I've explained it. When I hear them say, "I've heard people talk about this before, but I never understood it until today because you put it in a context that made sense to me," it shows me how important it is to use personal examples to convey a message. When I'm able to connect ideas in business with real-world situations and aid my team in comprehending that connection, there is nothing more satisfying than seeing the light bulb illuminate over their heads as they think, "I got it!" This knowledge empowers them to continue learning more independently. As a manager who sees such moments of understanding as my main goal, these words hold immense value for me.

FEAR VS. EMPATHY

Leaders, especially those in higher management positions, often fall into the trap of believing if they create an atmosphere of fear in their team, this will lead to more motivation and better results. I have personally seen and experienced this thought process too many times, but little do they know, this outdated mentality is far from the truth. Studies have shown employees who feel valued and supported produce higher-quality work, often faster and more efficiently than those who are fearful of making mistakes. Long-term performance improvement requires collaboration and supportive management techniques. Fear does not generate lasting motivation or commitment. Instead, it creates resistance and often leads to worse performance as staff becomes anxious and disengages from their work.

Whenever a manager shouts at their team and says heads are going to roll if they do not complete a project in a timely manner, it can be an intimidating experience for employees. In the moment, this type of response may seem appropriate, but managing staff in this way creates fear instead of understanding. Remaining empathetic during difficult times is essential to keeping the lines of communication open and ensuring positive progress toward the goal. Although creating some degree of fear can be necessary for certain situations, empathy should be at the forefront of any managerial approach.

In the mortgage industry, companies are overstaffed due to a decrease in loan volumes resulting from rising interest rates. To determine who to let go, some companies use a committee to review and rank employees, with the lowest-ranked employees being let go. Although I previously believed in this approach and still do to some extent, I knew I needed to modify my philosophy based on the facts of the situation. Instead of making quick, subjective decisions, I decided it would be better to take a few weeks to talk to employees and give them the opportunity to look for another job. If they found one, we agreed to still pay them their severance. Additionally, if an employee wanted to take a sabbatical, we could work with them to maintain their employment and benefits on a contract basis. Through this approach, I found most of the staff reductions I needed were achieved through voluntary departures, and it saved the company money while also keeping the remaining employees happy.

Because of this approach, numerous employees of mine were in great positions. During these circumstances, an employee of mine told me she was planning to quit her job to start a baking business. I supported her decision and asked her how long it would take for her to set everything up. She said it would take about three weeks. After three weeks, she came back to me and said her business was ready to launch, and she was ready to leave the company. I provided her with a severance package, which she used to fund the startup of her home-based kitchen for her special-event cookie business. Eventually, she expanded her business and opened a storefront with several employees. I am proud of the role I played in helping her achieve her dream, but I also acknowledge she did a lot of hard work to make it a success. Providing these types of opportunities and support is what management is all about.

It's important for managers and leaders to understand that their relationships with employees are truly beneficial on both sides. When employers recognize the long-term value they stand to gain in terms of lessons learned on how to better manage their staff, they can become more effective in their role as managers. Learning when and how to motivate team members or strategize efficiently are effective skills necessary to foster the positive work relationships between employer and employee and ensure better management and leadership qualities for longer-lasting success.

THOUGHT MANAGEMENT

- In what ways do you make yourself required in your current role within your company?
- How have you used sellable communication in your role and what were the results?
- Have you ever been managed in an atmosphere of fear? If so, how did it affect you and your team?

CHAPTER 8

EVALUATE SUCCESS

"Success is not final, failure is not fatal: It is the courage to continue that counts."

WINSTON CHURCHILL

The success of any organization can only be determined through an assessment of its performance and long-term goals. The process of evaluating success helps organizations identify areas of improvement and address potential weaknesses in their strategy or execution. By measuring performance accurately and analyzing the data effectively, organizations can better gauge the effectiveness of their efforts, allowing for more informed decisions about where to focus resources for maximum benefit.

INPUT & PEER REVIEW

When evaluating success, you need to determine what metrics should be utilized to accurately measure the successes as well as the trials and tribulations of the outcome. Outcomes will not always be perfect, so we cannot focus only on the factors predetermined to be successful.

When you're working on a project, you are going to go off course, and it's going to turn out different than you expected, but there are always positive or negative reasons for it. This is why you have to determine metrics upfront in terms of time, people, and resources. That way, when a project is complete, you can compare what you originally outlined with the outcome to determine what else you would have needed to do to be successful or what you still need to do to be more efficient in the future. Once measurable criteria are established and monitored, assessing a project's successes or failures becomes easier, which results in better decision-making for all involved.

Gathering input to evaluate what you've done is a crucial step in any successful endeavor because the human element should never be overlooked. Every level of the process needs input from those who thought of it, those who did it, and those who were impacted by the changes made or the successes that occurred. The most meaningful evaluations come from those closest to what you're doing, whether that's your customers or your employees, but third-party sources can also offer meaningful perspectives and insights to provide a full picture. The key to true understanding lies not only in gathering data but listening carefully to the stories surrounding it.

When I began working with the American Heart Association and helping out with their events, I was overwhelmed by the response from the organization itself. Knowing my involvement was making a major impact on a cause I deeply care about was truly inspiring. But I could not evaluate my work based solely on my opinion or the feedback from the organization. It was eye-opening to receive feedback from sponsors who had their own perspectives on how events and other endeavors turned out. Each of them had a unique way of gauging success and critiquing the event using their personal perspective and experience. It was remarkable seeing such varied reactions in regards to an effort I put my heart and soul into, and I was grateful for their feedback. Gathering opinions from sponsors allowed me to gain a clearer understanding of how others saw my project and how I could make adjustments for greater success in the future. Thanks to their input, we ended up exceeding our most optimistic expectations - and it was all worth it.

While it's important to get input, it needs to come from the right place because choosing the wrong individuals could prove to be detrimental rather than constructive. Never rely solely on the opinions of those in management because they often promote projects or changes with the hopes of being viewed as successful, no matter how it turns out. Whether as a result of vanity or the fear of failure, it clouds their judgment and makes it difficult to get an unbiased review.

Everyone has opinions, and some employees aren't shy about expressing them. Receiving input is invaluable, but filtering it can be difficult when feelings of criticism or unwarranted advice emerge. A valuable skill in any environment is the ability to recognize the difference between valid criticism aiding our development and mere harping. If individuals are only focusing on their personal shortcomings, there are techniques for ranking their most significant areas of improvement and understanding when their input has validity.

We all come in contact with situations in a work environment where the story is not completely told, so you have to either subjectively or objectively figure out what is missing. If you don't do that, you run the risk of missing important elements that could add to or distract from the process of what you're trying to accomplish. By probing for feedback, you can understand what is right under the surface that may be a shortcoming in management, in production, or in individual roles. Too many times, people don't ask questions, which causes tunnel vision in businesses. If you are only asking questions about four out of the eight critical elements of a project, you're going to miss a major component or have an overall project failure because you failed to account for all the elements of success. If a manager assumes their employees know all the information without vetting them to ensure understanding, that's a major oversight that can have disastrous effects in business.

Evaluating success is a challenging task. It takes courage to look back on your work and pinpoint where you may have made mistakes. However, it is also an important step in growing and improving yourself and your processes. To help make things easier, you have to ask yourself, "What could I have done to make this quicker, better, faster?" Doing so allows us to evaluate our performance fairly and honestly before setting out on the next endeavor or project.

FEEDBACK

Getting genuine, valid, and helpful feedback can sometimes be challenging, especially for managers, because employees will sometimes just tell them what they think they want to hear. Unfortunately, that's not helpful. As a manager, it's your responsibility to determine the best way to gather feedback from your team, and there are a few different options for doing that including group meetings, questionnaires, surveys, and one-on-one conversations.

Group Meetings

Group meetings are used to connect with the employees who are affected by the changes. When I'm trying to solicit feedback, I do it in two different ways. First, I meet with each group without any other managers present. This allows me to create a space where teams feel comfortable expressing their true feelings without their bosses in the room. Employees are more open and honest with this approach. Then, I bring some of the managers and those who supervise into a meeting with a few contributors from the team. It's important for everyone to have their say and be heard equally. This way, all opinions will be properly represented before we move forward with any changes.

At the meetings, I start off by expressing what's important about reaching our goal. I might say something similar to:

> *Striving for perfection is impossible, but constantly making improvements is within our reach. We've had a successful start, and I feel confident, having heard all the*

input from those of us in attendance, that we can make this task even more effective if we listen to the feedback and refine our process as we continue. Every day brings an opportunity to do better than before, and I believe, with the resources and abilities we have here, nothing should stand in our way. Let us do justice to this task by relentlessly refining it as far as possible.

I've had to learn over the years that even when sponsors are seemingly generous and well-intentioned, they don't always have the whole picture in mind. Unfortunately, I have seen some instances where actions taken out of good faith can lead to negative outcomes for another department or the customer. As a result, it has become my responsibility, as a leader, to advocate for many stakeholders and be able to look beyond what most employees see on the surface. Navigating these problems requires an open and honest dialogue between everyone involved and a clear understanding of how choices impact individual lives and work efforts. To facilitate lasting and meaningful change, we must continuously evaluate how each of our decisions affects all parties concerned.

Working together in teams can often be challenging, especially when projects require the coordinated action of multiple individuals. By holding group meetings for evaluations and getting everyone on the same page within an organization, you create a space for collaborative problem-solving and innovative solutions. This allows you to become more successful in achieving organizational tasks, reinforcing teamwork, and strengthening relationships through meaningful conversations. Each evaluation acts as a bridge between each team member's individual effort, ultimately unifying them together in pursuit of common goals.

Questions

Asking questions is one of the most powerful tools in any process, especially when it comes to getting feedback. It's the best way to proactively identify and effectively address potential issues before they become a problem. Being inquisitive about any situation can open the door to innovative solutions, meaningful dialogue, and deeper insight into what may be necessary for successful completion. Questions are valuable when it comes to problem-solving because they unravel layers of complexity in a straightforward and understandable way. Questions can even open the path toward profound change while inspiring critical thinking among those taking part, so don't underestimate their power when working through projects.

Creating short, verbal questionnaires can be extremely helpful in verifying understanding and fostering better communication, which encourages mutual involvement from all participants in the conversation. This is an invaluable technique, especially when discussing difficult topics that call for careful consideration of all concerned. Taking just a few moments to ask questions and clarify comments can help keep complex conversations on the right track and ensure all parties are on the same page.

Having your team not understand what you are saying can be incredibly disheartening and challenging, but it's always possible to improve and get buy-in from the employees in the room. Start by getting their feedback to see if your thoughts or ideas resonated with them. You could try breaking into small groups, giving each group one issue to focus on, and allowing them to connect, explore, and explain why they think it is important. This will help them better understand your point of view and build a stronger connection between team members.

Once the meeting is over, ask yourself what went well, what areas could have been improved, and who were your biggest helpers throughout the project or task. Analyzing what worked and what didn't work will help make future projects more successful. The key to implementing any change is to ensure all parties fully understand and buy in to what you're telling them. By listening to feedback from attendees and making new learnings your priority, you can ensure each one continues to be a better experience than the last.

Surveys and Ballot Boxes

Surveys provide an efficient and cost-effective way of acquiring honest, unbiased responses from customers to inform decisions made daily. When customers feel they're being heard, they will remain loyal to the organization and likely become advocates by recommending their favorite products and services with enthusiasm. Organizations cannot afford to underestimate the power of good customer service in this day and age, so surveys are a key part of ensuring customer satisfaction, which is the foundation for any successful venture.

Gathering feedback from your employees can also be incredibly important when it comes to making decisions and improving the workplace. Surveys give everyone a voice, so business owners can take the opinions of each employee into consideration on issues such as job satisfaction, working conditions, and organizational health. By listening to those who are closest to the operations of the business, meaningful changes can be made to create an even better work environment where everyone feels valued and motivated. Hearing their voices can spark increased commitment and satisfaction among the entire workforce, leading to greater productivity and success.

Polling your team on important matters is even easier. With silent ballots, you can quickly obtain feedback and see if your team is happy or not. It's also a way to get a clear vision of whether your initiatives have been successful or if you need to modify them. To make it even simpler, limit voting to just a "yes" or "no" response, so it's impossible to misinterpret the feedback. Polling is an opportunity to ensure everyone's voices of approval and disapproval can be heard, no matter how quiet they may seem.

Having a Conversation

Talking to your team can be the most powerful way to get their feedback on a project. It's important to listen closely and pay attention, as you may hear valuable insights to help propel your ideas forward. One simple way to do this is by casually walking around the office and talking with your team. Exchange ideas, try out creative solutions, and ask how they would approach an upcoming challenge. When we take the time to talk to our team, it can foster a close-knit relationship to move forward together. This approach does not require any extra time, effort, or resources. It relies on simple human connection, which is something each and every one of us desires. Give it a try for a few weeks, and watch your team flourish.

Evaluation through feedback is a crucial step to understanding the effectiveness of an organization's operations. It provides crucial insight into how it works, as well as potential areas where adjustments or sweeping changes can be made. However, it can sometimes be difficult to determine when adjustments should be made versus when a total overhaul should happen. The answer usually lies within the data and findings from the evaluation process. If there are major problems, then it's worthwhile to make some larger changes that may require more effort and resources. But, if only minor issues arise from the evaluation results, simply making some necessary adjustments could be enough to make a positive difference in the organization. No matter what decisions you have to make when evaluating your organization, it's important to stay informed on what processes and strategies will yield the greatest results.

INDIVIDUALIZED FEEDBACK

Employees need a roadmap to stay on track for success. In any given situation, there are multiple factors contributing to an individual's ability to reach their goals. Sometimes, they need more commitment and buy-in, while other times, they require additional support from their team to get the job done. With careful consideration and thoughtful action, it's possible to identify the unique steps each employee must take to become more successful. To accurately assess where an individual stands and point them in the right direction, ask yourself the following questions:

- How can we adjust our approach to provide a clear path for success and improvement?
- Is there a need for increased buy-in to the program?
- Is there a requirement for a higher-quality product?

- Is there a need for employees to provide better support and effective feedback to their team to improve teamwork?

- What actions can be taken to enhance the value of employees and enable their participation at work?

As a leader, it is incredibly important to provide your team with an environment that encourages and embraces change. This atmosphere of trust, respect, and open-mindedness will empower them to accept the alterations and be motivated enough to make these changes on their own. This creates a safe space where they can voice their opinions without fear of backlash and an environment that offers possible solutions and open dialogue about any challenges or hesitations regarding the transition process. Together, you can foster an environment where ideas are shared collaboratively and constructive feedback is given without judgment, so your team can work together as a unified force in bringing about this necessary change.

FREQUENCY OF FEEDBACK

Without taking a pause to assess how our efforts are translating into results, it's easy to become overwhelmed and not see any progress at all. However, when taken too often or without context, evaluations can take away from the progress we're trying to make by wasting valuable energy and resources on data that may not be adding any real value. While it's important to use feedback tools as part of our plan for success, they need to be used judiciously so we can continue pushing forward without getting stuck in the loop of over-evaluating.

Employees and Processes

Evaluating employees and their job performance is an incredibly important part of managing a successful organization. We all recognize measuring success is necessary to understand how individual team members are driving towards our goals, but not too frequently or too little. Too frequent evaluations can create a negative environment filled with anxiety and competition. Likewise, not conducting evaluations often enough removes the opportunity to quickly address any issues that arise in an employee's performance, which defeats the purpose of why we track performance in the first place. Yearly and quarterly evaluations are critical because they create a balance in the frequency of feedback. You will need to get your evaluation schedules on track so everyone in the organization can benefit from better support and feedback.

Companies often review employees only when the last quarter's financial performance isn't so great, and most companies are reluctant to give pay rises when they don't have the money for it. This is a big mistake. Rewards should be given when due, even if it puts some strain on your budget. Performance reviews are more meaningful and accurate if they are conducted on an employee's anniversary date, rather than in line with your fiscal calendar. Celebrating anniversaries and rewarding employees accordingly will ensure they feel appreciated for their hard work throughout the year, rather than just at year-end. Giving them the respect and appreciation they deserve by remembering all the efforts made throughout their year-long journey directs focus to what really counts – their overall performance. Everyone loves a pat on the back for a job well done, but extra money in their wallets goes a long way as well.

Examining the daily operations, workflow, and processes of an organization is necessary for its growth and success. Seeing where each team member or department stands in terms of completing their tasks is vital, but it does not need to be done all the time. Assessing every once in a while ensures no major issue remains undetected for too long, while being too involved can sometimes slow down the actual process.

Again, there needs to be a balance between being closely monitored and not overbearing enough to cause disruption. Taking a look at how things are being carried out paves the way for better productivity and motivates employees to take the initiative to overcome a challenge. Keeping tabs on what's going on in your organization on a regular basis will enable its success in the long run.

Products and Services

When you have worked hard to create a product or service you believe will benefit the lives of your customers, getting feedback can be both exciting and daunting. It is an opportunity to step back, reflect, and understand how well your creation has been received by others. This feedback can guide you on how to further improve what you offer in order to reach a wider audience. Obtaining feedback on products or services is critical for companies to remain competitive, so they can continue to improve upon the offerings they are providing to their customers.

As a customer, it can be incredibly exciting and fulfilling to see a brand respond quickly and positively to customer feedback, and it is the responsibility of organizations to take this seriously. Surveying customers shortly following implementation can provide brands with invaluable insights into how their customers felt before the service could be adapted or improved upon. Understanding this concept will give you the unique ability to garner customer loyalty through effective communication, evidenced by the quality of your product or service. Implementing customer surveys immediately after releasing an offering shows customers their opinions have tangible value and can make all the difference in creating lasting relationships with customers.

Constant evolution is an essential part of any successful business, meaning changes to websites and other marketing platforms should be embraced by businesses. Making adjustments to your website can open up a wealth of opportunities for hearing from customers and understanding which aspects of the website are working well and which need improvement. Putting in the effort to engage with customers and be receptive to their feedback will create a lasting impact on how your business progresses. As customers, we appreciate when our voice is heard and valued.

It's natural to worry employees won't like our products or services or think they are as great as we do. This is why it's all the more important to make sure even negative responses are taken into consideration. Listening and responding to what your customers say allows you to better understand their needs and expectations about your product, which will ultimately lead to stronger customer relationships and improved outcomes. When asking for feedback, aim for positive results but use unfavorable remarks as an opportunity to further refine and modify your product to give your customers what they want.

As a business, staying up-to-date with the latest opportunities provided by competitors is also essential for success. Without information gleaned from customer feedback and communication of new products developed by competitors, one risks missing out on potential further developments in the industry and any potential advantages or investments that could be made. Customers can provide businesses with valuable insight to keep them ahead of the competition or remain competitive in a continuously developing market. Gathering customers' feedback is driving many successful companies today and should be taken seriously when striving for growth and maximum reach.

Believe it or not, sometimes it is easy to miss the potential for products to be used for multiple purposes, but this is where customer feedback comes in. It may sound trivial, but recently someone discovered a product initially designed to polish copper that could also be used on the bottoms of frying pans. The company had never even thought of this, but after giving it a test drive and confirming its effectiveness, this new use put them at the top of their market. Utilizing hidden benefits like this can make all the difference in product performance. You never know what strangely compatible uses customers may stumble upon in their everyday lives. This goes to show the power of customer feedback.

FAILURE TO GET FEEDBACK

One of the biggest failures in management today is the failure to evaluate. If you don't have an evaluation process, you are likely to make the same mistakes over and over again. We manage the second ship the same way we managed the first, then we manage the third one the same way as well. We fail to learn from the different environments we are in, from our experiences in prior situations, and the pluses and minuses were in that environment. Sometimes, you will have managers who don't really understand the value we contributed to the company or why we should be rewarded for that value. When you're doing an excellent job for yourself, for the company, and for the customer, you deserve to be rewarded, and an evaluation process can ensure that.

Collecting meaningful customer feedback can be one of the most difficult parts of running an effective product operation. Despite investing time, effort, and resources into designing surveys to capture users' thoughts and feelings on a product, sometimes it can all feel like a waste when you don't get the feedback you were anticipating. It is incredibly frustrating when you've put in so much to hear nothing back, leaving your team feeling deflated and uncertain about future decisions in the work environment, but this doesn't have to be the case. With the right strategy in place, it's possible to generate the insights and metrics needed to ensure products continue to improve.

When I was in charge of a financial services company, I needed to ensure our new process for handling payoffs was effective and customer-friendly. I decided to hire a secret shopper company to gather feedback from our former customers, who I had trouble getting a response from using our traditional process. The old process required customers to either send in a written request, which would take three weeks, or fill out the request online with an electronic signature. The secret shopper company had a unique way of contacting customers, either through direct calls or emails followed by calls, and they were able to obtain a response rate of 5-6%. I provided them with the names and phone numbers of customers who had recently made an inquiry, and I had them ask six or seven questions specifically designed to obtain the necessary feedback.

When the secret shopper called one of the customers, they were pleased with the new process and said it was the fastest process they had ever experienced. I gave the secret shopper company about 100 customers to check up on. The cost was high, but it was worth it for the feedback, which proved we needed to establish a more effective way for our customers to communicate with us. Based on this feedback, we enhanced our website usability and even provided customers with incentives to complete questionnaires.

Seeking out valuable customer feedback can be a game-changer for any organization. With the right innovative methods, even those who aren't responding to traditional feedback sources can be surveyed, giving your organization a wider view of customer opinion. Spending money on these services can feel intimidating at first, but when viewed as an investment instead of an expense, the value of customer feedback becomes so much greater. Remember, what you put in now will lead to greater long-term growth. Take the plunge and make it part of your organization's success story.

PROMOTE YOUR SUCCESS

It's disheartening to watch employees put in incredible amounts of hard work for a project or initiative that goes on to be a great success, only for everyone to shrug it off as though nothing extraordinary has been achieved. Celebrating successes, big and small, is fundamental for fostering a sense of camaraderie and team spirit within any organization and is essential for creating an environment of positivity and motivation. It not only shows how much we appreciate what our colleagues have achieved but also serves as a reminder these successes have enabled us to move ever closer to realizing our collective goals. If we don't take the time to stop and reflect on the places where we've come together as a team, then all the efforts made become meaningless.

Celebrating success and achievement within an organization can be such an exciting way to encourage team spirit, collaboration, and unity. Achieving goals and developing skills boosts morale and can make a difference in how you are perceived by your peers and customers. There are many ways you can promote and celebrate your team's success in the workplace including weekly recognition for team members who have done an outstanding job or hosting luncheons or events where everyone is acknowledged for their hard work. These gestures show excellence is valued and encourage further growth. Seeing your entire team take pride in their accomplishments will be the best reward of all.

THOUGHT MANAGEMENT

- What have been the most successful ways you have been able to obtain feedback from your employees or customers? Why?

- How do you ensure customer surveys provide you with valuable and relevant feedback?

- During your journey through this book, what is your most impressive new realization you have had in regard to your work environment, your staff, and yourself?

CONCLUSION

"Yesterday is now gone, learn from it. Today is here, grow
from it, for tomorrow may never come."

H. MARC HELM

It would be foolish to expect success in every venture we attempt.
Sometimes, we miss the mark entirely. It is undeniably difficult to
face failure, but if left unchecked, it can become the norm. You, your
managers, and your staff should fully understand failure is not what
is expected or accepted. Everyone should have a willingness to fix
any broken processes, practices, or pieces within the organization.
Nothing will be perfect, but long-term failure is not acceptable.
When something doesn't go as planned, turn it into a learning
experience and get it right or better the next time. Use this mentality
to encourage your team to persevere through the challenge of fixing
mistakes and watch how it will strengthen your organization. Rather

than sweeping mistakes under the rug, they will be acknowledged and met with solutions.

The cliche, "If it ain't broke, don't fix it" is one of the most frustrating management expressions. This antiquated notion has held back progress across countless companies and industries, as it encourages employees to leave any existing process, product, or personnel issue exactly as it is. If there are significant opportunities for improvement, change is a vital part of any successful organization's growth and maturation. Oftentimes, organizations become stagnant as they fail to recognize the importance of embracing change. It's no longer acceptable not to strive for continuous improvement. Whether something is already working perfectly, or it could use some tweaks, taking a fresh look at what's been done before with an eye towards improving outcomes should be at the top of every organization's list of priorities.

So why not try replacing this notion of "fixing" things with "enhancing" them? One of the best ways to move a system forward is to continually enhance and repair it. When it comes to making your organization a better version of itself, taking small steps toward progress is often the best way forward. To master the art of self-evaluation, an organization needs to understand its strengths and weaknesses by utilizing feedback collected from various stakeholders internally and externally. Only then can the right adjustments be made to move the organization forward. We need to invest our time, money, and resources to become one percent better every day. Through continued effort and incremental improvements, it is possible for us to achieve true success.

These are principles I wholeheartedly endorse, practice, and strive for when managing people, projects, or initiatives. By objectively, holistically, and strategically viewing our environment, anything can be moved from average to excellence with proper focus and dedication. If I have served any purpose in this book, I hope it will help you become a better person, employee, and leader who contributes and takes initiative on all relevant opportunities to make a positive impact on everyone and every process that you encounter.

Embarking on this journey requires honesty, courage, trust, and confidence, all of which are found in our readiness to accept change, as it is only through change that true progress can occur. Without change, we risk letting opportunities pass us by and losing out on our potential for greatness. The world is your lock. "Preparing for Greatness" is your key.

ABOUT THE AUTHOR

H. Marc Helm is a modern-day Renaissance man with over forty-five years of management and leadership experience. Marc has built many successful companies and now dedicates himself to helping other owners grow strong businesses.

Marc Helm's unique perspective on business comes from his background in sociology and psychology, which he applies to his work as a business leader and author. He believes that success is not just about achieving a goal, but it's a journey that requires a commitment to personal growth and a willingness to learn from mistakes.

www.ingramcontent.com/pod-product-compliance
Lightning Source LLC
Chambersburg PA
CBHW030520210326
41597CB00013B/977